AF847474

Understanding Financial Risk Tolerance

Caterina Cruciani · Gloria Gardenal ·
Giuseppe Amitrano

Understanding Financial Risk Tolerance

Institutional, Behavioral and Normative Dimensions

palgrave
macmillan

Caterina Cruciani
Department of Management
Ca' Foscari University of Venice
Venice, Italy

Gloria Gardenal
Department of Management
Ca' Foscari University of Venice
Venice, Italy

Giuseppe Amitrano
WieldMore Investment Management
London, UK

ISBN 978-3-031-13130-1 ISBN 978-3-031-13131-8 (eBook)
https://doi.org/10.1007/978-3-031-13131-8

© The Author(s), under exclusive license to Springer Nature Switzerland AG 2022
This work is subject to copyright. All rights are solely and exclusively licensed by the Publisher, whether the whole or part of the material is concerned, specifically the rights of translation, reprinting, reuse of illustrations, recitation, broadcasting, reproduction on microfilms or in any other physical way, and transmission or information storage and retrieval, electronic adaptation, computer software, or by similar or dissimilar methodology now known or hereafter developed.
The use of general descriptive names, registered names, trademarks, service marks, etc. in this publication does not imply, even in the absence of a specific statement, that such names are exempt from the relevant protective laws and regulations and therefore free for general use.
The publisher, the authors, and the editors are safe to assume that the advice and information in this book are believed to be true and accurate at the date of publication. Neither the publisher nor the authors or the editors give a warranty, expressed or implied, with respect to the material contained herein or for any errors or omissions that may have been made. The publisher remains neutral with regard to jurisdictional claims in published maps and institutional affiliations.

Cover illustration: © John Rawsterne/patternhead.com

This Palgrave Macmillan imprint is published by the registered company Springer Nature Switzerland AG
The registered company address is: Gewerbestrasse 11, 6330 Cham, Switzerland

To our loving families

Preface

This book focuses on the contribution of financial risk tolerance in shaping the workings of financial markets. It takes a bold approach combining very different views to understand how this concept, lying at the crossroads of different domains of study and practice, including financial regulation, scholarly studies, and financial advisory practice, has been formalized over the last 30 years.

The book looks at the feedback loop among the different domains in which risk tolerance is assessed and operationalized to reorganize the current stream of research on financial risk tolerance and suggests further relevant domains in which a new risk tolerance definition will need to be defined.

Using key landmark moments in the normative evolution of financial services in the European Union including the introduction of the Markets in Financial Instrument Directive (MiFID) and its successor MiFID 2, this book will try to highlight the relationship between scholarly definitions of risk tolerance, key measurement tools, and the formal requirements imposed by regulatory institutions to key market players.

This book provides a snapshot of the most important dimensions in which financial risk tolerance has been analyzed and highlights the relationship between policy-making and scientific endeavor. We touch upon precursors of financial risk tolerance, reviewing key socio-demographic variables that have been found to affect it, and move on toward more dynamic versions of financial risk tolerance that include the role of life events. The different chapters focus on the debate on financial risk tolerance in specific time frames marked by regulatory events and provide an in-depth overview of two important changes in European financial markets—sustainable investment and fintech and robo advisory. A practitioner's view section authored by the CEO of a UK-based investment firm is included as a commentary and includes relevant insights from the world of financial advisory tied to the academic debate discussed in the text.

This book represents a valuable contribution to both the academic and the professional debate as it brings together different streams of literature in a critical review, exploring the feedback loop between academic research and financial practice to draw insights on the regulatory future of financial services.

Venice, Italy — Caterina Cruciani
Venice, Italy — Gloria Gardenal
London, UK — Giuseppe Amitrano

Acknowledgments

The idea to write this book stems from the thought-provoking and fruitful discussions between persons with different jobs but a similar passion for knowledge and understanding.

Bringing together a practitioner with decades of experience and two academic scholars studying financial markets and institutions was our way to prove that contamination between different approaches is the best way to look at ever-changing concepts like financial risk tolerance. As financial markets continue to evolve, there is a profound need for open discussion and exchange of ideas and we hope that this book provides useful material in this respect.

A very important part of this book could not have been written without the support of Federico Melotti and Andrea Papoff at Wield-More Investment Management, who organized and chaired the webinar in which we launched the practitioners' questionnaire discussed in the last chapter of this book. Caterina Cruciani and Gloria Gardenal wish to thank Giuseppe Amitrano and all the WieldMore Investment Management team for believing in the soundness of the project and for helping in the promotion of the survey among practitioners.

The list of acknowledgments would not be complete without mentioning our supporting and loving families. Writing a book is no easy feat and we all owe the biggest thank you to our spouses and children, who cheered us along the process, provided inspiration, and much-needed entertaining breaks and to whom this book is dedicated.

Contents

About the Authors

Caterina Cruciani is Assistant Professor in Financial Markets and Institutions at the Department of Management, Ca' Foscari University of Venice, where she also received a Ph.D. in Economics. She is the Operating Director of the Center for Experimental Research in Management and Economics (CERME) and a member of the Risk-Lab at Ca' Foscari University of Venice. Caterina's research interests focus on behavioral finance, financial advisory, and SME financing. Caterina teaches Financial and Banking instruments, Corporate banking and Behavioral Finance at the University of Venice and in professional training activities for financial advisors. Caterina provides regular updates on her latest publications, achievements, and research interests on the main professional social networks (LinkedIn, Academia.edu, ResearchGate) and on Twitter.

Gloria Gardenal is Associate Professor of Corporate Finance and a member of the Risk-Lab and the Center for Experimental Research in Management and Economics (CERME) at Ca' Foscari University of Venice, where she also received a Ph.D. in Business. Her research focuses on corporate finance, risk management, and investment decisions, with a particular interest in behavioral finance. She taught several Bachelor's and Master's courses including Corporate Finance, Valuation, Financial Policies and Investment Strategies and also has been involved in more advanced courses like M.B.A. in Finance and International Finance. She is present on the social networks (Facebook and Twitter) and in all the main professional social networks (LinkedIn, Academia.edu, ResearchGate) where she promotes her published work and academic achievements.

Giuseppe Amitrano is the Chief Executive Officer at WieldMore Investment Management, London UK. A leading expert as Head of Trading and Sales, senior Managing Director in rates and credit derivatives with over 25 years of experience, Giuseppe has created and led fixed income derivatives teams at Scotiabank, RBS and UBS where he has been running absolute and relative return strategies. He has been board member of the Corporate Social Responsibility Committee of Scotiabank Europe, London. Further to his M.Sc. in Economics he obtained the CISI Level 4 Investment Advice Diploma in 2018.

List of Figures

List of Tables

CHAPTER 1

Financial Risk Tolerance: Where Does It All Start From?

Abstract This chapter introduces the relevance of the debate on financial risk tolerance starting from reconstructing the key macroeconomic changes that progressively expanded the investor base in Europe and beyond starting in the 1990s, focusing both on financial markets and on other relevant sectors. The increased investment opportunities available to the retail investor expanded potential opportunities for financial gain for individuals but also highlighted the need to provide clear guidelines to structure and shape these opportunities considering all the risks. The need to govern this important change in financial markets favored the convergence of different disciplines on the importance of financial risk tolerance: regulation, academia, and practitioners were all called upon figuring out how to measure this somewhat elusive concept. This chapter focuses on the period prior to the introduction of the Markets in Financial Instruments Directive (MiFID) in Europe when financial advisory was not yet considered a proper financial service and investors were still transitioning from direct holdings of stock to more flexible tools like mutual funds. Besides briefly describing the regulatory framework, a literature review of risk tolerance measurement and drivers is provided, to conclude with a practitioner's view regarding the relevance of risk tolerance measurement in this period.

Keywords Mutual funds · Risk tolerance drivers · Financial knowledge

© The Author(s), under exclusive license to Springer Nature Switzerland AG 2022

C. Cruciani et al., *Understanding Financial Risk Tolerance*,
https://doi.org/10.1007/978-3-031-13131-8_1

1 A Crossroad: Why Looking at Risk Tolerance?

Starting in the 1990s a combination of factors set the stage for a major convergence of the interests of very different disciplines toward the activities within financial markets and their implications for the different actors involved. While economists had been interested in why individuals should engage in financial markets for decades drawing mixed messages, financial institutions developed and started offering new investment opportunities available to most of the population in developed countries. Financial markets became more necessary as public policies started to change; contribution-based pension reforms and massive privatization waves in key utilities rightly attracted the attention of many. The importance of new professional figures changed as markets started drawing the attention of less financially literate individuals in need for advice and guidance and not only financial products. The combination of all these factors finally attracted the attention of the regulator, interested in shaping this transition while protecting the interests of all. This section reviews these major changes starting from the traditional economic view on stock-market participation and discusses the macroeconomic changes and the regulatory implications they brought about.

1.1 The Economists' View

Financial risk tolerance is a key element in the determination of investment choices that has consequences both on current and future consumption: the level of risk tolerance is likely to determine how much liquidity is steered toward saving or investing, reducing the liquidity available for current consumption to increase it in the near or distant future when the investment bear its results.

A natural starting point for this analysis is understanding why and how financial risk tolerance matters is asking why individuals should invest in the financial system. Despite providing numerous opportunities and services, financial markets expose individuals to artificial risks with the promise of returns that are governed by the laws of probability rather than by natural laws they are accustomed to.

One starting possibility is that participation in financial markets yields positive results for society as a whole. In this context, a large literature developed on **stock-market participation and wealth**. While the macroeconomic literature is not conclusive on whether increasing stock-market participation improves general welfare (Basak, 1996; Black, 1974; Errunza & Losq, 1985, 1989; Eun & Janakiramanan, 1986; Stulz, 1981; Subrahmanyam, 1975), a key finding is that increases in stock-market participation do not necessarily reduce wealth inequality in the population in the medium run. Individuals differ along a variety of relevant dimensions and their attitudes and propensities make them enter and exit the stock market at different times: more risk averse, less financially educated individuals are drawn to participating in market upswings but tend to leave the stock market in the downswings and be replaced by larger stockholders. Thus, despite larger participation, individual wealth inequalities are not necessarily reduced (Bilias et al., 2017).

Individuals feel differently about risky investment, but classic portfolio analysis suggests that those interested in utility maximization might want to hold at least some stocks, as they indisputably yield higher returns, provided that the portfolio is properly constructed (Arrow, 1994). Thus, even risk averse individuals may take on some risk provided that it is correctly managed.

In the 1990s the empirical evidence focusing on stock-market participation showed that despite this theoretical consideration there were individuals who did not invest in stocks with major differences across countries. Guiso et al. (2003) show that total participation in financial markets ranged from 54% of individuals in the United States to 15% in Italy and explain these diverse patterns by discussing entry costs into the stock market related to the supply of more affordable financial products or to the pressure to plan for the future due to institutional changes in the pension systems. Guiso and colleagues conclude that individual differences in households (especially in terms of risk aversion and financial education) are a key factor to monitor the long-term implications of larger participation.

1.2 *The Macroeconomic Perspective*

The 1990s represent a very interesting decade for stock markets all over the world that affected the direct and indirect entry costs: among the first group, we find changes in market supply (both in terms of quantity and quality) that differentially affected the United States and Europe. Indirect entry costs were shaped by changes in neighboring sectors that will be discussed shortly.

For what concerns supply, a general trend, that affected countries all over the world, regards the wave of privatization of public utilities that brought to the market well-known stocks with a large potential investor base. Already started in the late 1970s, the privatization of State-owned enterprises saw almost 2500 deals in 121 countries being concluded over the period 1977–1999 for a net worth of over 1110$ billion (Bortolotti et al., 2004). Privatizations benefit from more liquid stock markets that can accommodate larger issues easily, increasing the speed and size of the revenues. Using a panel of 34 countries over the 1977–1999 period, Bortolotti and colleagues empirically show that privatization waves tend to exploit hot market periods: the increase in the extent of privatization activities thus signals that domestic stock markets have already become more liquid.

In terms of direct entry costs, the blossoming of the mutual stock fund industry finally brought to investors easy access to well-diversified products, helping the transition from direct acquisition to fund subscription (Guiso et al., 2003). The growth in the mutual fund industry was remarkable all over the world: between 1992 and 1998 the average annual growth rate of US mutual funds was over 22.4%, while European funds grow by an annual rate of 17.7%. The development of equity mutual funds was stronger in the United States than in Europe where bond funds were more popular (Fernando et al., 2013). Mutual funds are naturally targeted to households looking for a good level of diversification with a relatively low level of fees and commissions: individual investment is pooled and invested in very diversified funds, whose policy is defined in advance and is not subject to the preferences of the investors participating in the fund. While mutual funds require well-developed securities markets, where market integrity and liquidity are high (Fernando et al., 2013), they also have the potential to enlarge the investor base to less financially educated individuals, who might otherwise refrain from investing (Guiso et al., 2003). The overall effect of these trends is that new entrants—less educated than experienced stockholders and with fewer financial means to face the stock-market fluctuations—will influence the behavior of excess returns on equity, as education tends to correlate negatively with risk aversion (Guiso & Paiella, 2018).

Another macroeconomic factor that supported the increased pace in the regulation of financial markets to support the demand for financial products is that improved levels of well-being led to the progressive aging of the population in many countries. Economists were already puzzled by the evidence that many individuals tend to save too little to ensure a similar standard of living after retirement (Bernheim et al., 2000). This evidence was abundant, especially in the literature regarding the United States, where individuals were already called upon to make important decisions regarding their pension during their working life. For instance, Bernheim finds that individuals undersave for retirement as they tend to hold too optimistic expectations regarding their future wealth, do not possess an adequate level of financial literacy—the ability to understand and use correctly key notions in economics and finance—and do not have access to high-quality guidance in making financial decisions (Bernheim, 1998). While the author called for more effective financial education programs, later evidence has shown that such programs have at best a limited effect. Collins et al. (2010) find some positive effects in 41 programs but highlights that any attempt at evaluating such programs suffers from a self-selection bias, as one cannot rule out that only the more motivated individuals sign up. Often the effect of these programs is limited to some decision domains such as savings and barely distinguishable from what happens in control groups (Miller et al., 2015); moreover, the decay is as rapid as 20 months after the program is complete (Fernandes et al., 2014). An increase in life expectancy has the potential to magnify the scale of this pension unpreparedness with a major impact on the economy. At the same time, the 1990s saw the beginning of a transition from defined-benefit to defined-contribution welfare systems in Europe, which further increased the need for efficient financial planning for retirement even in countries where stock-market participation was low.

1.3 The Regulator's View

At the European level, the 1990s brought about a new wave of legislation that supported the creation of the common financial market and initiated shaping the features of investment services and investor protection and regulating the responsibilities of the different market actors.

Following the introduction of the Single European Act in 1987 (European Commission, 1987), the Maastricht Treaty formalized the structure of the internal market and established that free movement within the European Union should extend beyond people, goods, and services to capital as well. The Treaty formally established the European Union, set the stage for the introduction of the Euro as the Union's common currency, and created the banking Union with the Single Supervisory Mechanism (Treaty on the European Union, 1992).

Free movement of capital[1] extends from real investment and purchases to security investments of all kinds, reducing the frictions and the entry costs into any market within the European Union.

Investment services in this new operational landscape are regulated by another landmark document in European history: the Investment Services Directive (ISD) in the securities field, introduced in 1993 (European Commission, 1993). The Directive provides clear definitions of key investment services and investment tools and defines rules for offering these services in the Union introducing some key concepts regarding the supply of financial services that will remain crucial in EU legislation to come. The Directive has two key goals: setting up the rules of conduct and practice for banks and investment firms to ensure free movement of capital and strengthen the Union, and "to protect investors" while taking "account of the different requirements for the protection of various categories of investors and of their levels of professional expertise" (Preamble, p. 2).

Concerning **investment firms**, the Directive clearly describes the process through which they may be authorized to operate in a Member State and includes financial products under the umbrella of the principle of mutual recognition, by which all investment firms that are authorized in one Member State are allowed to do so in others "as long as they do not conflict with laws and regulations protecting the general good in force in the host Member State" (Preamble, p. 2). Title V of the Directive defines more closely the rules regarding this mutual recognition that require investment firms to either establish a branch in the Member State where they wish to provide investment services or operate directly if they already have the authorization for those services in their own Member State.

The Directive spells out clearly the "conditions for taking up business" in the Union (Title 2), and the necessary requirement an investment firm needs to possess to be authorized are included in Article 3, where both

[1] Any restrictions on the free movement of capital in the EU will be then safeguarded also in the other key document forming the constitutional basis for the European Union, the Treaty on the function of the European Union (Treaty on the Functioning of the European Union, 2012), which states it explicitly in Article 63 and extends also to payments (Art. 63 point 2).

financial soundness and good reputation are necessary (Article 3 point 3). Supervision of the quality of the financial players in the European market is further ensured by the Directive, which lays out both prudential rules and rules of conduct for the market players: in fact, Article 10 discusses the "prudential rules which investment firms shall observe at all times" (p. 10) that include internal control practices and sound accounting procedure, but also careful record-keeping and care to prevent conflict of interests between firm and clients or between clients.

Article 11 lays out the broad architecture for the **rules of conduct**,[2] ranging from the integrity and competence of the investment firms to the importance of discussing with the clients their "financial situations, investment experience, and objectives as regards the services requested" (p. 11). More importantly, Article 11 marks the first step in the pursuit of what will become a longer-term effort of the European legislator in disciplining the provision of financial advice and the distinction between different categories of investors. In fact, the article explicitly states that the rules of conduct need to be applied keeping in mind the "professional nature of the person for whom the service is provided" (p. 11) setting the stage for the now well-known distinction between retail and professional clients.

The need to formalize the distinction between **sophisticated and retail investors** is one of the key points regarding investor protection that is called for in another landmark document in the history of financial services in the European Union. The Financial Services Action Plan (FSAP), introduced in 1999 (Commission of the European Communities, 1999) laid out three objectives for the European common capital market, namely establishing a strong, single wholesale market, making retail financial markets open, and strengthening the prudential supervision. The FSAP recognized that the process of harmonization within the Union was not yet complete and that the Investment Services Directive needed to be improved. It is notable that once again, alongside more precise rules for the involvement and operating of investment firms, the Action Plan mentions explicitly the need for consumer protection. In

[2] Although these rules apply to all services, the Directive includes financial advisory as a non-core service in Annex C and clearly states that investment firms that only provide financial advice may not receive authorization to operate: "Authorization within the meaning of this Directive may in no case be granted for services covered only by Section C of the Annex" (Article 3).

particular, the Plan mentions that any obstacles to the integrated market should be removed to ensure that consumers have access to increased choice and competitive terms, to build and support trust. The Plan calls for the clarification of the "essential requirements" at the heart of the EU financial legislation, highlighting that "a high consumer protection" should be at their basis (p. 16). The Plan calls explicitly for clear rules for business conduct in terms of sophisticated and retail investors since Article 11 did not provide a criterion to distinguish between different professional nature of clients but help in this respect was provided by the Forum on European Securities Commission (FESCO) in March 2000.

FESCO brings together the securities regulators of the countries of the European Economic Area (EEA) to provide their experience and support to coordinate action toward the implementation of the Single Market and is instrumental in the discussion and elaboration of common standards to regulate financial services in areas where legislation did not provide proper harmonization guidelines (Demarigny, 2000). For what concerns the application of Article 11 of the ISD, FESCO provided precise criteria to identify professional investors (FESCO, 2000) focusing on the needs and professional competence of the client as required by the ISD. The criteria suggest that professional investors require a less stringent degree of protection considering their professional qualifications. Two categories of entities are classified as professionals: the first includes entities that are required to be authorized to operate in the provision of financial services in the EU (such as credit institutions and investment firms) and national governments and central banks; the second one includes large and institutional investors which must explicitly request to be treated as professional clients. The first category may also request to be treated as a non-professional client and have access to a greater degree of protection in the conduct of business.

A year later FESCO published another paper commenting on the application of Article 11 to address the lack of harmonization in business conduct across the different Member States to ensure an equivalent degree of protection throughout the EEA, improve investment flows in the EEA and promote cooperation between competent authorities in terms of conduct rules (FESCO, 2001). The paper asserts the principle that all investment firms must act honestly fairly and correctly, delegating to other firms only when professionally relevant and engaging in interaction with authorized firms only (Principle 1). Investment firms must communicate clear, fair, and not misleading information that should be sufficient to make relevant decisions (Principle 21). The information provided should regard both the investment firms (Principles 33 and 34) and the financial instruments and products (Principles 36 and 37). It is noteworthy that the FESCO principles and rules dedicate an entire section to "Risk warnings," suggesting that the information provided regarding risk should be pertinent not only to the financial investment but also to "the client's knowledge, experience, investment objectives, and risk profile" (Principle 53, p. 18). An entire section of the paper is devoted to the Know-your-client principle, covering investment objectives, risk profile, financial situation/capacity, trading restrictions, the identity of the clientele, and the suitability of the investment product provided (Sect. 3). This section presents clear rules to perform client analysis, which include "types of services, transactions, and products the client is familiar with and his trading history, i.e., the nature, volume, frequency and timeframe of his transactions" (Rule 72, p. 21) and "temporal horizon of the client's investments, as well as his preferences regarding risk-taking, profitability, and recurrent earnings" (Rule 73, p. 21), while there is no clear guidance as to how to obtain information about the client's financial situation and capacity, which should be "sought as appropriate in the context of the services rendered" (Rule 74, p. 22).

The joint effort of the ISD, the FSAP, and the FESCO papers clearly paint the picture of the investor protection that the European regulators have in mind in terms of broad contents, but there seems to be no indication as to the form in which this information needs to be collected.

2 Trends in Financial Risk Tolerance

The previous sections described the backdrop in which participation in financial markets started increasing, highlighting that well-functioning and liquid capital markets were crucial both to address endogenous changes in population dynamics and to cement the new monetary Union that was taking shape in Europe in the 1990s. The regulatory effort was aimed at drawing the general rules of conduct of the different players, laying the foundations for mutually fruitful interaction between investors and investment firms, while at the same time smoothing out the differences in business practices and investment products that existed in a yet not fully harmonized European financial market.

While the key concepts of consumer protections were laid out, a great degree of flexibility in their translation into actual practices was allowed.

Clear goals without as-clear directions might have been then informed by the large and growing literature on financial risk tolerance coming from empirical academic studies. The goal of this section is to summarize the key insights coming from scientific work regarding risk tolerance definitions and measures to understand the degree of interaction between the regulatory needs to address risk tolerance for investor protection and the scope of academic research. Given the importance of the MiFID Directive in shaping the measurement in financial risk tolerance, all the evidence presented in this chapter dates before its introduction, leaving to Chapter 2 to pick up on this literature review for the years that follow.

2.1 Definitions of Risk Tolerance

Academics have defined financial risk tolerance differently over time. A generally accepted definition is "the maximum amount of uncertainty that someone is willing to accept when making a financial decision" (Grable, 2000, p. 625). However, it is not the unique one. According to the prevalent literature at the end of the XX century (see, for example [Droms, 1988; Roszkowski et al., 1993]), there were few, if any, generally recognized measures designed to ascertain someone's financial risk tolerance or preference. There was a flourishing of "in-house" metrics created by financial planners of the time, but no one emerged as the standard by which the others could be evaluated.

The literature shows at least three diverse ways of defining risk tolerance: a "self-perceived risk tolerance" measure, which is usually measured by survey questions about the respondents' subjective risk tolerance (Grable & Lytton, 1998; Hanna & Chen, 1997), a numerical scale to represent the degree to which people are risk tolerant (Hanna & Chen, 1997) and, finally, as the ratio between risky financial assets to total assets or risky assets to net worth (i.e. objective risk tolerance). These varied ways of defining financial risk tolerance determined some inconsistencies in the analysis of its determinants that will be thoroughly described in the following sections. It is worth mentioning that, up to the year 2000, many studies focused on determining the attitudinal and personality factors affecting risk tolerance, while the socio-economic and demographic factors have been studied less extensively (Grable, 2000). After 2000, more studies have tried to systematize the findings concerning these factors, particularly after the MiFID in Europe. The following section summarizes key determinants of financial risk tolerance in the empirical literature grouping them into socio-demographic factors.

2.2 *Risk Tolerance Determinants*

2.2.1 *Socio-Demographic Factors*

This section reviews the key literature regarding the main socio-demographic determinants of risk tolerance in empirical literature, which include **age, gender, occupation, marital status and the presence of economic dependencies, ethnicity, financial education, and financial literacy**.

The evidence about the relationship between risk tolerance and **age** shows some inconsistencies mainly due to the use of different definitions for risk tolerance. Overall, most of the studies show a negative relationship between risk tolerance and age: older people appear to be less risk tolerant (Bajtelsmit & Bernasek, 1996; Chang et al., 2004; Grable & Lytton, 1998; Hawley & Fujii, 1993; Sung & Hanna, 1996; Wang & Hanna, 1997). A possible explanation for these findings is that older people have less time to recover losses, and for this reason, they become less tolerant of risks while aging.

Other studies showed mixed results: (Morin et al., 1983), for example, show that, on average, risk tolerance decreases as age increases. More specifically, risk tolerance decreases with age for households with a low level of net worth but increases with age for households with a high level of net worth. Wang and Hanna (1997) test the life-cycle hypothesis using data from the 1983–1989 Survey of Consumer Finance (SCF) panel and find that risk tolerance increases with age when other variables are controlled.

Another study that proves the opposite result is (Grable, 2000): using a random sample of faculty and staff (591 women and 484 men ranging in age from 20 to 75 years) working at a large US southeastern university in 1997, he finds that older people are more risk tolerant. As a possible explanation, Grable shows that taking into account possible interactions between and among the demographic, socio-economic, and attitudinal variables, a combination of education, financial knowledge, income, and occupation explained the most between-group variability in risk tolerance (about 22%), confirming that an extensive and systematic analysis of other demographic, socio-economic, attitudinal, and psychological factors might be used to differentiate among levels of risk tolerance more effectively, either individually or in combination. Moreover, he claims that understanding a person's financial risk tolerance is a complicated process that goes beyond the exclusive use of socio-economic factors and more research is needed in the domain of business and psychology (Grable, 2000, p. 629).

Another interesting result is provided by Chang et al. (2004), who show that in their sample age is related to objective risk tolerance (how people invest), but it is not related to subjective risk tolerance (what people say about their tolerance for risk). This may provide support for the necessity, on one side, that financial advisors help each client assess their risk tolerance and, on the other side, that they review the topic frequently because objective risk tolerance is likely to decline at some point.

Finally, other studies show that the general pattern of age seems to be that risk tolerance decreases with age after 45, which suggests that risk tolerance exhibits a hump-shaped pattern, i.e., it increases with age and then decreases. As proof of that (Hariharan et al., 2000) found that risk tolerant investors nearing retirement did not reduce their bond allocations in order to buy more stock.

Moving on to **gender**, the literature about financial risk tolerance and this factor is very broad. In the pre-MiFID era findings seem to be consistent and show that men are overall more risk tolerant than women (Bajtelsmit & Bernasek, 1996; Hawley & Fujii, 1993; Sung & Hanna, 1996).

Sung and Hanna (1996) look at differences in risk tolerance among single women, single men, and married couples and find that single women have lower risk tolerance with respect to both married couples and single men.

Chang et al. (2004) show some further evidence: using the 2001 Survey of Consumer Finances (SCF), they find that single women declare to have less tolerance for subjective risk, but there is no difference compared to couples regarding their investments. This might be due to the fact that some single women in the survey are widows or divorced and their assets might reflect their previous status as part of a couple. However, according to the authors, this evidence suggests that financial advisors should discuss risk tolerance with each client regardless of their gender. The authors also confirm the results by Sung and Hanna (1996) and find that couples are more likely to be risk tolerant than either unmarried women or unmarried men. Unmarried women appear to be less risk tolerant than unmarried men.

Occupation is another relevant driver in determining individuals' risk tolerance. According to many studies, being employed in a professional occupation is positively associated with risk tolerance (Grey & Gordon, 1978; Lee & Hanna, 1995; Leonard, 1995; Masters, 1989; Meyer et al., 1961; Quattlebaum, 1988). Haliassos and Bertaut (1995) as professional occupations guarantee higher wages on average and higher financial stability.

Sung and Hanna (1996) use the 6 categories of the 1992 Survey of Consumer Finance (SCF)—i.e., managerial and professional specialty; technical, sales, administrative support; service; precision production, craft, repair; operators, fabricator, laborers; farming, poultry, fishing—and find that households with a self-employed head tended to be significantly more risk tolerant than those that did not have a self-employed head. However, other occupation variables were not significantly related to risk tolerance controlling for other covariates, except for the actual risk tolerance for households headed by someone in a managerial/professional occupation, which was higher than those in other occupations, confirming the findings previously mentioned.

Grable and Lytton (1998) show that self-employed people (but also farmers in their sample) were significantly more likely to be willing to take risks than otherwise similar households with different occupations. Chen and DeVaney (2002), instead, comparing those who owned businesses and those who worked for someone else, found that risk tolerance was positively related to net worth for owners, but there was no significant relationship between risk tolerance and net worth for those who worked for someone else.

Overall, risk tolerance seems to be certainly higher for professionals and for those who are self-employed.

Changes in family structures have long been observed to produce variations in risk tolerance. These variations may be due to a variety of reasons: variations in preference elicitation methods, different definitions of risk preferences, different population studied, different methodological choices. Such variations are robust—they occur across different studies in a very similar manner. Moreover, it is important to point out that the robustness of these findings draws also from a theoretical appraisal of how changes in family structure may affect risk preferences. Disregarding the traditional expected utility framework, which has proven inadequate to address these risk preference variations, there are at least three other theoretical strands that provide support to the evidence we will soon describe (Chaulk et al., 2003). Getting married or having children may affect what an individual perceives as a basic need, thus producing choices that are seemingly not consistent with one's attitude to risk. This explanation is based on a hierarchical model of needs à la Maslow (1954): getting married may increase resources and help meeting basic needs more easily, making the possibility to meet secondary needs more likely. Alternatively, even prospect theory (Kahneman & Tversky, 1979; Tversky & Kahneman, 1992) offers a useful framework for interpreting changes in observed choices and underlying preferences when family structure changes. Getting married or having a child may change the mental frame that individuals use to assess gains and losses, producing choices that are, once again, seemingly inconsistent with previously observed ones. Last but certainly not least we may draw important insights from family development theory, which suggests that family changes bring about a change in expectations (both personal and societal) and in the potential for future changes. Interestingly, family development theory theoretically predicts why having a first child brings about more marked changes in risk preferences than any other following child or why men and women may change their risk preferences differently despite facing the same event (e.g., marriage and parenthood). Chaulk et al. (2003) highlight the connection between prospect theory and family development theory, with the latter providing the aspirational level over which gains and losses are defined over time.

Exploring the role of **marital status**, increasing levels of risk tolerance have been associated with being single (Baker & Haslem, 1974; Lazzarone, 1996; Roszkowski et al., 1993; Sung & Hanna, 1996). Married couples have a more conservative approach with respect to risk-taking but results also depend on the size of the households. Results in this regard are mixed. For example (Sung & Hanna, 1996) find no relation between the size of households and risk tolerance. They find no significant differences among households of different sizes when other variables were controlled, although the actual level of risk tolerance was lower for households with 5 people than for other sizes. On a different note (Grable & Joo, 1999) show that size of households matters: the higher the dependencies, the lower risk tolerance.

Another driver of risk tolerance in empirical analysis is **individual ethnicity**. Around the end of the Nineties, the United States started to be concerned about Blacks being less involved in the financial markets with respect to Whites, thus missing the possibility to benefit from market gains (Boyce, 1998). For this reason, many authors started to investigate if that evidence could be the consequence of differences in risk tolerance driven by race or by cultural differences. Some of the studies have demonstrated that White non-Hispanic households tend to be more risk tolerant than Hispanics, both using subjective and objective measures of risk tolerance (Chang et al., 2004). Other studies have shown exactly the opposite: using a sample of 220 white-collar clerical workers, (Grable & Joo, 1999) find that non-White respondents tended to be more risk tolerant.

Sung and Hanna (1996) take a different perspective: they find that Hispanics were less risk tolerant than otherwise similar White non-Hispanics, but this fact might seem to reflect purely subjective differences. For instance, this result might reflect a purely cultural difference. Moreover, they claim that it is equally plausible that the difference reflects a lack of understanding of the nature of financial risk. It is also possible that the groups with predicted lower risk tolerance had more uncertainty about non-investment income, even though some objective factors such as occupation and education were controlled.

Gutter et al. (1999), using data from the 1995 Survey of Consumer Finance, develop a life-cycle savings model incorporating socio-economic, financial, and attitudinal variables that shows that the observed racial differences in the individual determinants of risky asset ownership are centered on the impact of children and household size. Having children in the household increases the likelihood of stock or business holdings for Black households. Household size is negatively related to risky asset ownership for Black households. The same variables do not have a statistically significant effect on White households. Moreover, the paper shows that there are no racial differences in the impact of the reported willingness to take risk through risky asset ownership, thus eliminating the prejudice that there are racial differences and Blacks perceive risks differently with respect to Whites.

Risk tolerance is also affected by two very important "dimensions" explicitly stressed by the EU Regulator in Principle 68 letter c of the 2001 Consultative Paper promoted by FESCO[3]: **financial education and financial literacy**. Individuals' knowledge of financial markets and products clearly represents a relevant dimension for the Regulator, who

[3] FESCO establishes that it is the responsibility of the investment firm to identify the most suitable products for its clients, after determining "***client's knowledge and experience in the investment field***, his investment objectives and risk profile, and his financial situation/capacity" (FESCO, 2001, p. 21).

considers it a key aspect to determine the suitability of the financial products promoted by the investment firms.

Financial knowledge can arise from three main sources: education, “field experience,” and specific financial education programs. Looking at education, many studies in the pre-MiFID era investigated the relation between this driver and the attitude toward risk-taking. Hawley and Fujii (1993) using the 1983 Survey of Consumer Finances analyze the relationship between net worth and individual characteristics on risk tolerance and find that education, income, and debt were positively related to risk tolerance. The same pattern of relation is confirmed also by Warner and Cramer (1995), Lee and Hanna (1995), and Sung and Hanna (1996), using different survey data. The relation is confirmed also considering different measures of risk tolerance. For example, Chang et al. (2004) use both objective and subjective risk tolerance measures and find that as the level of education increases, risk tolerance increases as well. More specifically, households with only a high school education or less were the most likely to indicate no tolerance for risk.

However, financial knowledge cannot be simply approximated by education but may be affected by experience in the field. Chen and Volpe (1998) found that a large percentage of college students were not knowledgeable about personal finances. A 20-question survey of 1467 mutual fund investors conducted jointly by *Money* magazine and the Vanguard Funds Group showed that most investors had inadequate knowledge about their mutual fund investments (Updegrave, 1996). In a survey commissioned by the Investor Protection Trust (Crenshaw, 1996) less than one-fifth of all individual investors (in stocks, bonds, funds, or other securities) could be considered “financially literate” based on their responses to a quiz.

Alexander (1998) examine responses from a survey of 2000 randomly selected investors in mutual funds (the OCC/SEC survey) and develop their own measure of financial literacy. Their results show that the average investor’s score is five out of nine. Moreover, investors purchasing directly from fund companies scored much higher than any other fund group. Broker and pension plan purchasers also scored significantly higher than those buying mutual fund shares through other distribution channels. However, bank and insurance company purchasers received significantly lower mean quiz scores than other survey respondents. Authors also examine respondents’ financial literacy results together with several demographic and financial characteristics differentiated by the number of channels used to buy mutual funds. They discover that multiple-channel purchasers have significantly higher financial literacy scores than those who used only a single channel (5.70 vs. 4.44, respectively), with the largest difference being in the pension channel (5.78 vs. 4.21). The average quiz score was higher for males and for those respondents who work in the financial services industry and generally increased with age, education, and income. Finally, they investigate the sources of information used to get knowledge about the investments and find that respondents who reported that financial publications and the prospectus were the best sources of information scored significantly higher in financial literacy. In contrast, those who relied on family or friends, bank representatives, employer-provided printed materials, and insurance company representatives scored significantly lower.

The evidence just reported triggered the emergence of new mandates for national governments to educate and protect financial consumers (OECD, 2005). Therefore, regulators began to promote financial literacy education, attempting to change how consumers behaved and empowering them to reduce barriers to market participation and improve the accessibility of relevant information (e.g., Cartwright, 2004; Fox et al., 2005; Howells, 2005). According to this perspective, financial education works in concert with consumer protection measures to improve decision-making skills and enables individuals to make use of remedies such as disclosure and reflection rights. It is within this framework that many studies tried to investigate and measure individual financial knowledge and to discover their relations with financial risk tolerance.

Among academics, financial knowledge started to be identified with two distinct expressions: financial education and financial literacy. Financial literacy can be defined as measuring how well an individual can understand and use personal finance-related information (Huston, 2010). Financial education mainly refers to the education programs that can be offered to individuals to increase their financial literacy.

Many studies run on high school students consistently found that they were not receiving a good education in personal financial fundamentals and had poor knowledge (see for example, Bakken, 1967; Langrehr, 1979). In a study of 1509 high school seniors from 63 schools, Mandell (1997) reported an average correct score of 57% in the areas of income, money management, savings and investment, and spending. His conclusion was that students were leaving schools without the ability to make critical decisions affecting their lives.

2.2.2 *Economic Factors*

This category encompasses studies that address the role of **income, wealth, and retirement**.

Income is a good predictor of risk tolerance and results are pretty consistent: overall, increased levels of income are associated with higher risk tolerance (Baker & Haslem, 1974; Cicchetti & Dubin, 1994; Cohn et al., 1975; Grable & Joo, 1999; Lee & Hanna, 1991; Masters, 1992; Schooley & Worden, 1996; Shaw, 1996; Zhong & Xiao, 1995).

According to Malkiel (1996), the risk that an individual can afford to take depends on the total financial situation, including the types and sources of investment income. Hanna and Chen (1995) use an expected utility and simulation approach to derive optimal portfolios, based on risk aversion and the ratio between a household's financial investment portfolio and total **wealth**, including human wealth. They show that this ratio is important to determine what level of volatility is optimal for a portfolio, and that ratio would tend to be related to such objective factors as years until retirement. Based on plausible assumptions about risk aversion and the actual distribution of the ratio of financial assets to total wealth in the United States (Lee & Hanna, 1995) find that it would be rational for most households to have only stocks in portfolios intended for long run goals such as retirement. For younger workers investing for retirement, willingness to accept some risk (volatility) would lead to substantially greater wealth at retirement (Chen & Hanna, 1996).

Risk tolerance affects individuals' willingness to invest in the financial market. This fact influences both the current amount of invested wealth but also how much money individuals will have at their disposal at **retirement**. Sung and Hanna (1996) try to understand how risk tolerance is related to the number of years until expected retirement and find that those who are 30 years or more away from retirement have significantly higher risk tolerance than otherwise similar respondents whose expected retirement was closer. Instead, Bernheim (1998) stresses an important issue discussed earlier: individuals undersave for retirement as they tend to hold optimistic expectations regarding their future wealth, do not possess an adequate level of financial literacy, and do not have access to high-quality guidance in making financial decisions. While the author called for more effective financial education programs, later evidence has shown that such programs have at best a limited effect. Hariharan et al. (2000) use a large individual-level data set to isolate the effects of risk tolerance on portfolio composition. They test and confirm two predictions of the Capital Asset Pricing Model: (1) increased risk tolerance reduces an individual's propensity to purchase risk-free assets; and (2) higher risk tolerance does not affect the composition of an individual's portfolio of risky assets. More specifically, they find that risk tolerant investors nearing retirement do not reduce their bond allocations to buy more stock.

2.2.3 Personality Psychology

For many years, academics have investigated the personality factors affecting financial risk-taking. One personality factor found to be linked consistently with financial risk-taking is **sensation seeking** (Wong & Carducci, 1991; Zuckerman, 1983; Zuckerman et al., 1978). Sensation seeking is "the need for varied, novel, and complex sensation and experiences and the willingness to take physical and social risks for the sake of such experiences" (Zuckerman, 1979, p. 10). Wong and Carducci (1991) use the concept of sensation seeking—which was proved to be positively related to risk-taking associated with gambling—to investigate if it can be extended to everyday money matters. Among the various results, the authors show that high sensation seekers within each gender group tend to take greater risks with everyday money matters. So, high-sensation-seekers women take more risks than the low-sensation-seeker ones. Furthermore, males were observed to engage in greater financial risk-taking than females irrespective of their sensation-seeking scores.

Another personality factor associated with risk-taking behaviors is the **Type A behavior pattern** (cf. Haynes & Matthews, 1988). This behavioral pattern is characterized by individuals who are hard-driving and competitive, with an underlying tendency for hostility and aggressiveness, and a heightened sense of time urgency and impatience (Friedman & Rosenman, 1974; Houston & Synder, 1988; Strube, 1991; Thoresen & Low, 1990). This behavioral pattern has been found to be associated with a tendency to maximize achievement in situations involving intellectual and physical pursuits and a willingness to take extended personal risks to do so (Carver et al., 1976; Haynes & Matthews, 1988; Howard et al., 1977; Lovallo et al., 1986; Matthews & Siegel, 1983; Mettlin, 1976; Sorenson et al., 1987; Weidner & Matthews, 1978). However, this research has not investigated how such willingness to take personal risk can translate to situations involving personal finance. Some general implications for the Type A pattern in mediating willingness to take financial risks is based on factors like the generally competitive nature of Type A individuals and their concern for achievement (Houston & Snyder,

1988; Strube, 1991; Van Egeren et al., 1982). In their attempt to achieve economic success, the Type A behavior pattern is associated with a willingness to take greater risks in everyday financial matters than that of the Type B behavior pattern. Moreover, as Type A individuals tend to possess a higher income level than Type B individuals (Thoresen & Low, 1990), such financial security might make it possible for Type A individuals to be willing to take greater financial risks than Type B individuals. In their study, (Carducci & Wong, 1998) analyze Type A and B individuals and find that Type A subjects are significantly more risk tolerant than type B. This can be explained by the tendency of Type A individuals to be generally more competitive and concerned with personal achievement (Ray & Brozek, 1980) and to be recognized in an industrial society (Houston & Synder, 1988). Type A subjects care a lot about their financial success, as it is used by society to identify a successful person. Since financial success is proportional, in a sense, to the financial risk taken, Type A individuals would be more willing to take greater financial risks to achieve financial success and be recognized as successful by society. The tendency of Type A individuals to possess a higher income level than Type B individuals (cf. Thoresen & Low, 1990) is another possible reason for their willingness to take greater financial risks than Type B individuals.

The following table provides a summary of all the papers mentioned organized by topics and subtopics (Table 1).

2.3 *Measurement Tools*

The role of risk attitudes in shaping individual decision-making has been a major theme in economic literature from the earliest models of decisions under uncertainty onward. Despite the centrality of risk tolerance for the definition of an appropriate financial plan, a generally agreed-upon measure of this concept was still lacking in that decade. Notwithstanding this, the empirical effort in measuring risk tolerance spurred a lot of research in economics, finance, and psychology literature. The financial planning literature proposes a categorization of the tools used to measure risk aversion that includes choice dilemmas, utility theory, objective measures, heuristic judgments, and subjective measures (Grable & Lytton, 1999). In consumer research literature three different methodologies to assess risk preferences are present: choice dilemmas, gambles, and self-reported measures (Mandrik & Bao, 2005). The economic theory uses different metrics within the Expected Utility framework

Table 1 Factors influencing financial risk tolerance—an academic view before MiFID

Variable	*Effect*	*References*
Age	Negative relationship	Bajtelsmit and Bernasek (1996), Chang et al. (2004), Grable and Lytton (1998), Hawley and Fujii (1993), Sung and Hanna (1996), Wang and Hanna (1997)
	Positive relationship or U-shaped pattern	Chang et al. (2004), Hariharan et al.(2000), Morin and Suarez (1983)
	Positive relationships	Grable (2000)
Gender	Males are more risk tolerant than females	Bajtelsmit and Bernasek (1996), Hawley and Fujii (1993), Sung and Hanna (1996)
	Gender and marital status	Sung and Hanna (1996)
Occupation	Type of occupation (being a professional or a self-employed)	Chen and DeVaney (2002), Grable and Lytton (1998), Grey and Gordon (1978), Haliassos and Bertaut (1995), Leonard (1995), Lee and Hanna (1995), Masters (1989), Meyer et al. (1961), Quattlebaum (1988), Sung and Hanna (1996)
Marital status and child dependencies	Being single increases RT	Baker and Haslem (1974), Lazzarone (1996), Roszkowski et al. (1993), Sung and Hanna (1996)
	Size of household (mixed findings)	Grable and Joo (1999), Sung and Hanna (1996)
	Changes in family structure affect risk tolerance	Chaulk et al. (2003), Tversky and Kahneman (1974, 1992)
Ethnicity	White non-Hispanic households tend to be more risk tolerant than Hispanics	Chang et al. (2004)

(continued)

Table 1 (continued)

Variable	*Effect*	*References*
	Hispanics are more risk tolerant than non-Hispanics	Grable and Joo (1999)
	Ethnic differences have no effect on risk taking	Gutter et al. (1999), Sung and Hanna (1996)
	Personal characteristics	Bernheim (1998)
	Portfolio composition and RT	Hariharan et al. (2000)
Financial education	Positive relation with RT	Chang et al. (2004), Hawley and Fujii (1993), Lee and Hanna (1995), Sung and Hanna (1996), Warner and Cramer (1995)
Financial literacy	Positive relationship with RT	Bakken (1967), Cartwright (2004), Chen and Volpe (1998), Fox et al. (2005), Howells (2005), Langrehr (1979), Mandell (1997)
Income and wealth	Higher income determines higher RT	Baker and Haslem (1974), Chen and Hanna (1996), Cicchetti and Dubin (1994), Cohn et al. (1975), Grable and Joo (1999), Hanna and Chen (1995), Lee and Hanna (1991), Malkiel (1996), Masters (1992), Schooley and Worden (1996), Shaw (1996), Zhong and Xiao (1995)
Retirement	Years until retirement	Sung and Hanna (1996)

Variable	*Effect*	*References*
Personality psychology	Sensation seeking and Type A behavior pattern	Carducci and Wong (1998), Carver et al. (1976), Friedman and Rosenman (1974), Haynes and Matthews (1988), Houston and Synder (1988), Howard et al. (1977), Lovallo et al. (1986), Matthews and Siegel (1983), Mettlin (1976), Sorenson et al. (1987), Strube (1991), Thoresen and Low (1990), Van Egeren et al. (1982), Weidner and Matthews (1978), Wong and Carducci (1991), Zuckerman (1983), Zuckerman et al. (1978)

theory, but also the risk-return framework typical of finance is used, while decision theory and psychology focus also on psychometric scales (Betz et al., 2002). The different approaches have different focuses but overall managed to establish a series of important results to build upon in the following decades. The following sections will try to provide an organized overview of the different tools put forward before the advent of the MiFID and discuss the approach and the merits of each of them. As the review will show, elicitation methods matter: the way in which risk preferences are assessed may lead to different results.

This section will discuss the merits and limitations of the key categories of tools used to measure financial risk tolerance, focusing on whether the measures tend to be purely descriptive or if they somehow advance knowledge in understanding the process of risk aversion in this domain.

2.3.1 Choice Dilemmas

Such tools present individuals with a series of choices framed in risky scenarios conditions and use decisions to infer risk preferences. The validity of the constructs used to define the choice dilemmas determines their ability to accurately measure risk aversion. Choice dilemmas were very popular in the 1970s, but their results are not stable. For instance, Cartwright (1971) finds that allowing for group discussion changes the risk assessment of such scales, and (Grable & Lytton, 1999) suggest their popularity has diminished due to the one-dimensionality of the risk questions. This type of approach focuses strictly on revealed behavior and does not control for the perception of benefits and risks associated with the different scenarios presented.

2.3.2 Expected-Utility-Based Tools

Utility theory tools are based on specific models of decisions under uncertainty that allows determining how risk aversion should be measured. Consider for instance the Expected utility Theory model, which uses a well-behaved utility function to determine individual attitudes toward risk. Given the shape of the utility function and gambles over the real space a risk averse individual would always find the expected value of playing a random gamble to be preferred to the random gamble itself. Using this notion, individual choices can be observed, risk profiles clearly classified, and the shape of the utility function determined with clarity for everyone. Moreover, the observation of individual choices would explain why people choose differently: e.g., a risk averse individual would prefer a much smaller certainty equivalent than a risk-neutral person not to play a gamble. The first problem with such a theory is that according to the method used to measure utility (in certainty-equivalent or in probability-equivalent ways) individuals tend to be classified differently (Slovic, 1964). The well-known phenomenon of preference reversal shows the dramatic implications of procedure variance (Tversky et al., 1990): when choosing between a large probability of winning a small sum (H-bet) or a small probability of winning a large sum (L-bet), most people prefer the former. When asked to state their lowest selling price for the two lotteries, the L-bet is marked higher than the H-bet. The inconsistent patterns emerging from different methodologies to assess risk profiles within the expected utility framework have been the subject of several empirical analyses both in economics and psychology and it would be beyond the scope of this paper to review them in full. Nevertheless, it is important to point out that systematic deviations in empirical studies fueled the development of alternative models of decision-making such as the previously mentioned prospect theory, which, among its many other key contributions, established the existence of a change in risk profile between the domain of gains and of losses. The fact that risk preferences are not stable within the same individual and using a common medium (monetary gains or losses) reduces the viability of expected-utility-theory-based tools to determine risk tolerance, although it has the merits of trying to discuss the process of risk evaluation. The economic literature, especially the experimental one, has proceeded to couple traditional revealed-preference approaches with belief-elicitation procedures to assess directly unobservable attitudes (for a review see [Schotter & Trevino, 2014]). Reviewing this literature is beyond the scope of this book, although it is important to note that the effectiveness of such techniques in eliciting true beliefs is still discussed (see for example [Danz et al., 2022]).

A similar approach trying to use formal frameworks to derive financial risk tolerance is the risk-return framework. A prominent feature of this approach is that it allows modeling the process behind risk aversion by using the basic framework used in finance to trade off expected benefits with risk, commonly measured with an asset's variance in finance. Moving to psychological risk-return models allows us to assume that perceived risk instead of variance determines the riskiness of the underlying asset, and to allow it to vary across contexts. The introduction of perceived risk allows reconciling some of the apparently inconsistent choices observed for instance in choosing prospects across gains and losses as observed in prospect theory.

2.3.3 *Objective Measures*

These measures are based on actual holdings of stocks or other risky assets in individual portfolios; the larger the share of stocks, the higher the tolerance for risk. There are several issues with this procedure: on one side, it assumes that the proportion of stocks in the individual portfolio actually and correctly represents the individual risk aversion and is not mediated by third parties. Moreover, and more importantly, it assumes that portfolio composition is a perfectly rational act (Grable & Lytton, 1999). Empirical evidence from behavioral finance shows that portfolio composition is unlikely a purely rational act: even as markets become more and more interconnected investors tend to select stocks prevalently from their own country (French & Poterba, 1991), and this home-bias phenomenon is true even when considering the choices of mutual fund managers (Coval & Moskowitz, 1999). Even if some individuals do not rely on financial advisors or third parties, the existence of strong behavioral biases in investing prevents the mere observation of the share invested in stocks in their portfolios from providing a full and clear picture of risk tolerance, making these tools descriptive rather than predictive and not able to understand the process behind risk aversion. Moreover, focusing on choices made these measures cannot account for risk perceptions, and thus do not go from conventional risk tolerance to perceived-risk tolerance.

The Health and Retirement Survey[4] in the United States collects information about the investment composition of respondents (e.g. amount allocated in stocks) and allows to derive an objective measure of financial risk tolerance that has often been used in empirical analysis in combination with many other health-related and attitudinal variables collected.

2.3.4 *Heuristic Methods*

This method is reportedly used by finance professionals and is based on the empirical findings linking socio-economic characteristics and observed risk tolerance (Grable & Lytton, 1999). A key problem is

[4] The questionnaire documentation is available at this link https://hrs.isr.umich.edu/documentation/questionnaires.

that the theoretical literature up to the mid-1990s seemed unable to describe accurately the relationship between risk aversion and some socio-economic features, such as age where different theoretical models predict different (increasing and decreasing) relationships between aging and taking risks (Yoo, 1994). The applicability of such heuristic models thus lies in exploring further the likely non-linear relationship between individual characteristics and risk (Grable & Lytton, 1998) rather than being able to shed light on the risky decision-making process per se.

2.3.5 Self-Reported/Subjective Risk Measures

Subjective measures of financial risk have been collected in large-scale survey of consumers and investors across the world. Popular choices include the Survey of Consumer Finance (SCF) for the United States, the German Socio Demographic Panel (SOEP) and the Survey on Health, Aging and Retirement in Europe (SHARE), whose subjective risk questions are included in Table 2.

One prominent advantage of relying on such measure is that these surveys are conducted over long time intervals over representative samples of the population, allowing for large-scale studies with meaningful implications. On the other hand, self-reported survey answers are not incentive compatible, thus forego some of the advantages of performance-based incentivization that other forms of individual assessment have (Camerer & Hogarth, 1999) to improve performance in economic experiments. Nevertheless, empirical research lends support to the fact that self-reported measures are reliable in assessing risk attitudes. Dohmen et al. (2011) explored whether subjective measure positively relates to more objective ways to elicit financial risk tolerance finding and finds that self-reported risk attitudes correctly predict risky choices in a real-stakes lottery experiment, confirming the validity of survey-based measures. Hallahan et al. (2004) compare the risk tolerance emerging from a more complex Risk Tolerance Scale comprising 25 items and self-reported assessments and find that the two measures are generally in agreement: this confirms that how people feel about risk and how they act upon it seem to be two connected processes.

2.3.6 Risk-Behavior Scales

Another popular choice is the use of more complex financial risk tolerance scales. Scale are composite tools that allow to consider the multifaceted nature of financial risk tolerance instead of relying on only one dimension.

Table 2 Subjective measures of financial risk tolerance from large-scale representative surveys

Survey of consumer finance (SCF)	*German socio demographic panel (SOEP)*	*Survey on health, aging and retirement in Europe (SHARE)*
Which of the following statements comes closest to describing the amount of financial risk that you are willing to take with your spare cash? That is, cash used for savings or investment Participants can choose from the following responses (emphasis not added) 1. I take substantial financial risks expecting to earn substantial returns. 2. I take above-average financial risks expecting to earn above-average returns. 3. I take average financial risks expecting to earn average returns. 4. I am not willing to take any financial risks. 5. I never have any spare cash. In the waves used in this study, people who choose option 5 are given the following follow-up question Assume you had some spare cash that could be used for savings or investment. Which of the following statements comes closest to describing the amount of financial risk that you would be willing to take with this money? They are then asked to choose from 1 to 4 above	Indicate on a scale from 0 to 10 how you see yourself in terms of your willingness to take risks, with 0 representing no tolerance for risks and 10 representing the greatest willingness to be exposed to risk	When people invest their savings they can choose between assets that give low return with little risk to lose money, for instance a bank account or a safe bond, or assets with a high return but also a higher risk of losing, for instance stocks and shares. Which of the statements on the card comes closest to the amount of financial risk that you are willing to take when you save or make investments? 1. Take substantial financial risks expecting to earn substantial returns 2. Take above-average financial risks expecting to earn above-average returns 3. Take average financial risks expecting to earn average returns 4. Not willing to take any financial risks.

Grable and Lytton (1999) highlight the key features of a valid and reliable measure of risk tolerance including specific dimensions of risk like the probability and size of gains and loss, the need to focus specifically on the financial domain and the trade-off between length and clarity. In the paper they introduce the Grable and Lytton risk tolerance scale and discuss how the 13-item tool was developed and validated.

Box 1.1 the Practioner View

In this box, Giuseppe Amitrano (WieldMore Investment Management) draws a picture of the financial markets in the pre-MiFID era, tackling the open issues discussed in this chapter

Did the booming market opportunities and the need to engage more people in financial markets justify the lack of formality regarding risk tolerance? Which rules existed? Was compliance (to what?) a key driver?

The booming performance of the market and a wider participation of investors in terms of age and wealth distributions only begun at the beginning of the 90s both in the U.S. and in Europe.

The historical series of the distribution of household wealth in the U.S. since 1989 shows that wealth was almost equally distributed between above and below 55 years of age ($11.13tn *versus* $9.29tn, respectively), a completely different situation with respect to nowadays, where the same distribution between over and under 55 years of age ($96.7tn *versus* $45.4tn) basically sees younger generations halving their participation to general wealth (Source: Board of Governors of the Federal Reserve System). The high wealth available for the working population in the 90s was favored, among other things, by the large increase in real estate value and the low-interest rates. The investors who fostered the necessary regulatory changes and modelled the current market environment are the same who experienced the ride from those days to today. The formality that followed regarding data transparency, suitability, and risk tolerance has been very helpful to develop market liquidity and confidence but has been also instrumental to secure those legacy positions.

During the 90s the existing rules were essentially the corporate laws and standard governance codes of conduct. They have been the first and most important sources of investors' protections for all financial institutions, as they were specified by the legal system. The use of contract laws provided the fundamentals of compliance for all deals, privately negotiated but also publicly arranged. All aspects of the company life, from foundation to bankruptcy, and to securities dealing were at the time regulated by laws affecting the right of both insiders and outside corporate investors. Therefore, the good functioning of the markets and the protection of investors developed at the same time with the capability of the different regulators and courts to guarantee and, if necessary, enforce these laws. The protection of corporate investors became the first step to create the confidence for attracting investments, and through financing companies, creating a well-functioning financial market.

Limits and checks have always been a characterizing trait of financial firms. The role of compliance has been more of a gatekeeper rather than a driver, but the concept that there was a defined area of operation and amount of risk-taking has always been present. However, in the very early days of modern financial markets, during the end of the 80s, the role of compliance was less relevant, in the sense that operativity was more flexible and implied less bureaucracy. Compared to nowadays, there was a more limited control from the regulators, performing less checks which created room for irresponsible management behavior (like MF, LTCM, and Lehman).

Was there a perception that investors were to be protected from or rather encouraged to take on risk? Based on what?

One of the main provisions in terms of investor protection was that investment firms must match the client's investment profile with suitable products. Today, the idea of suitability itself is to find a product and an overall portfolio that is tailored for the client himself/herself, like a suit. That means it should not push investors to take risks they are not able to bear. On the other hand, it is important that regulation does not create barriers where they are not needed, because that would imply a cost-opportunity situation. The core idea that led to the MiFID was to increase transparency to deliver the perfect suit for the client. Nevertheless, the bumpy rides financial markets faced during the early years probably moved the industry to look at risk through a more conservative lens, from a regulatory point of view. This resulted in the provision of a target market and compatible customers from the very beginning of the product life cycle.

3 Conclusions and Roadmap of the Book

The goal of this chapter was to set the stage for the remaining of the book. The major trends in financial markets characterizing the Eighties, Nineties, and early 2000 have been described, with the diffusion of the mutual funds' industry and, at the same time, the concern of governments and regulators about investors' protection. In fact, the low levels of financial literacy, the low participation in the financial market, and the tendency not to worry about the future and retirement of investors at the end of the XX century determined a generalized interest, both by academics and regulatory authorities, to better understand investors' behavior and risk tolerance when dealing with financial matters. In particular, the academic literature focused extensively on understanding the determinants of financial risk tolerance, considering demographics, socio-economic factors but also psychological traits. One of the criticalities acknowledged looking into the literature of that time is the variety of risk tolerance measures and scales, that determined mixed results on some of the drivers under analysis and the need to further investigate this issue.

In the next chapters, the book will describe the evolutions both at the regulatory and academic level of these issues, highlighting moments of discrepancy between the academic debate and legislative requirements and difficulties by the financial professionals to put into practice the regulatory requirements. In particular, Chapter 2 reviews the two major Directives in Europe—MiFID 1 and MiFID 2—and the contemporaneous academic debate about risk tolerance and investor's risk profiling; Chapter 3 introduces one of the major challenges the European regulator is currently facing, i.e., sustainability and sustainable investments, trying to shed light on how risk tolerance could be affected by sustainability and the implications on the professional ground; Chapter 4 introduces a second challenge, i.e., the digitalization of financial services, in particular, Fintech and Robo advisory trying to highlight how this revolution changes both investors' behavior toward financial services and the banking business model; finally, Chapter 5 concludes by presenting the results of survey of financial advisors.

References

Alexander, G. (1998). Mutual fund shareholders: Characteristics, investor knowledge, and sources of information. *Financial Services Review*, *7*(4), 301–316. https://doi.org/10.1016/s1057-0810(99)00023-2

Arrow, K. J. (1994). *Methodological Individualism and Social Knowledge.*, *84*(2), 1–9.

Bajtelsmit, V. L., & Bernasek, A. (1996). Why do women invest differently than men? *Journal of Financial Counseling and Planning*, *7*, 1–10. https://doi.org/10.2139/ssrn.2238

Baker, H. K., & Haslem, J. A. (1974). The impact of investor socioeconomic characteristics on risk and return preferences. *Journal of Business Research, 2*, 469–476.

Bakken, M. R. (1967). Money management understandings of tenth grade students. *National Business Education Quarterly, 36*, 6.

Basak, S. (1996). An Intertemporal Model of International Capital Market Segmentation. *The Journal of Financial and Quantitative Analysis, 31*(2), 161. https://doi.org/10.2307/2331178

Bernheim, D. (1998). Financial illiteracy, education and retirement saving. In *Living with Defined Contribution Pensions* (Issue 1996).

Bernheim, D. B., Forni, L., Gokhale, J., & Kotlikoff, L. J. (2000). How much should Americans be saving for retirement? *American Economic Journal: Applied Economics, 90*(2), 288–292.

Bilias, Y., Georgarakos, D., & Haliassos, M. (2017). Has greater stock market participation increased wealth inequality in the US? *Review of Income and Wealth, 63*(1), 169–188. https://doi.org/10.1111/roiw.12225

Black, F. (1974). International capital market equilibrium with investment barriers. *Journal of Financial Economics, 1*(4), 337–352. https://doi.org/10.1016/0304-405X(74)90013-0

Bortolotti, B., Fantini, M., & Siniscalco, D. (2004). Privatisation around the world: Evidence from panel data. *Journal of Public Economics, 88*(1–2), 305–332. https://doi.org/10.1016/S0047-2727(02)00161-5

Boyce, J. (1998). Blacks are bearish on Wall Street says new survey. *The Wall Street Journal, 231*(69), C21.

Camerer, C. F., & Hogarth, R. M. (1999). The effects of financial incentives in experiments: A review and capital-labor-production framework. *Journal of Risk and Uncertainty, 19*(1–3), 7–42. https://doi.org/10.1023/a:1007850605129

Carducci, B. J., & Wong, A. S. (1998). Type A and risk taking in everyday money matters. *Journal of Business and Psychology, 12*(3), 355–359. https://doi.org/10.1023/A:1025031614989

Cartwright, P. (2004). *Banks, consumers and regulation*. Bloomsbury Publishing.

Carver, C. S., Coleman, E. A., & Glass, D. C. (1976). The coronary-prone behavior pattern and the suppression of fatigue on a treadmill test. *Journal of Personality and Social Psychology, 33*, 460–466.

Chang, C.-C., DeVaney, S. A., & Chiremba, S. T. (2004). Determinants of subjective and objective risk tolerance. *Journal of Personal Finance, 3*(3), 53–67.

Chaulk, B., Johnson, P. J., & Bulcroft, R. (2003). Effects of marriage and children on financial risk tolerance: A synthesis of family development and prospect theory. *Journal of Family and Economic Issues, 24*(3), 257–279. https://doi.org/10.1023/A:1025495221519

Chen, Z., & DeVaney, S. A. (2002). What factors affect the household net worth of employees and business owners? *Financial Services Review, 11*(4), 381–391.

Chen, P., & Hanna, S. (1996). Retirement accounts: High returns with safety. In *Proceedings of the Association for Financial Counseling and Planning Education* (Vol. 107, p. 116).

Chen, H., & Volpe, R. P. (1998). An analysis of personal financial literacy among college students. *Financial Services Review, 7*(2), 107–128. https://doi.org/10.1108/JCM-01-2018-2514

Cicchetti, C. J., & Dubin, J. A. (1994). A microeconometric analysis of risk aversion and the decision to self-insure. *Journal of Political Economy, 102*, 169–186.

Cohn, R. A., Lewellen, W. G., Lease, R. C., & Schlarbaum, G. G. (1975). Individual investor, risk aversion and investment portfolio composition. *Journal of Finance, 39*, 605–620.

Collins, J. M., O'Rourke, C. M., & O'Rourke, C. M. (2010). Financial education and counseling-still holding promise. *Journal of Consumer Affairs, 44*(3), 483–498. https://doi.org/10.1111/j.1745-6606.2010.01179.x

Commission, E. (1987). EC: Single European Act. *Official Journal of the European Communities, 169/2*. https://doi.org/10.54648/taxi1986045

Commission of the European Communities. (1999). *Financial services: Implementing the framework for financial markets: Action plan*. http://ec.europa.eu/internal_market/finances/docs/actionplan/index/action_en.pdf

Consolidated version of the treaty on the functioning of the European Union. (2012). https://eur-lex.europa.eu/LexUriServ/LexUriServ.do?uri=CELEX:12012E/TXT:en:PDF

Danz, D., Vesterlund, L., & Wilson, A. J. (2022, in press). Belief elicitation and behavioral incentive compatibility. *American Economic Review*.

Demarigny, F. (2000). The Forum of European Securities Commissions (FESCO): An answer to the needs of a European single market for financial services. *Revue D'économie Financière (English Ed.), 60*(5), 125–133. https://doi.org/10.3406/ecofi.2000.4509

Dohmen, T., Falk, A., Huffman, D., Sunde, U., Schupp, J., & Wagner, G. G. (2011). Individual risk attitudes: Measurement, determinants, and behavioral consequences. *Journal of the European Economic Association, 9*(3), 522–550. https://doi.org/10.1111/j.1542-4774.2011.01015.x

Droms, W. G. (1988). Measuring investor risk capacity with a pass. *Journal of Financial Planning*.

Errunza, V., & Losq, E. (1985). International asset pricing under mild segmentation: Theory and test. *The Journal of Finance, 40*(1), 105–124. https://doi.org/10.1111/j.1540-6261.1985.tb04939.x

Errunza, V., & Losq, E. (1989). Capital flow controls, international asset pricing, and investors' welfare: A multi-country framework. *The Journal of Finance, 44*(4), 1025–1037. https://doi.org/10.1111/j.1540-6261.1989.tb02636.x

Eun, C. S., & Janakiramanan, S. (1986). A model of international asset pricing with a constraint on the foreign Equity ownership. *The Journal of Finance, 41*(4), 897–914. https://doi.org/10.1111/j.1540-6261.1986.tb04555.x

European Commission. (1993). Council directive 93/22/EEC of 10 May 1993 on investment services in the securities field. *Official Journal of the European Communities*, *L*, 27–46.

Fernandes, D., Lynch, J. G., & Netemeyer, R. G. (2014). Financial literacy, financial education, and downstream financial behaviors. *Management Science, 60*(8), 1861–1883. https://doi.org/10.1287/mnsc.2013.1849

Fernando, D., Klapper, L., Sulla, V., & Vittas, D. (2013). The growth of mutual funds. *World Bank Policy Research.* https://doi.org/10.1007/978-1-4302-6020-2_3

FESCO. (2000). *Implementation of article 11 of the ISD: Categrization of investors for the purpose of conduct of business rule.*

FESCO. (2001). *Standards and rules for harmonizing core conduct of business rules cover note. 0*, 1–52.

Fox, J., Bartholomae, S., & Lee, J. (2005). Building the case for financial education. *Journal of Consumer Affairs, 39*(1), 195–214.

French, K. R., & Poterba, J. M. (1991). Were Japanese stock prices too high? *Journal of Financial Economics, 29*(2), 337–363.

Friedman, M., & Rosenman, R. H. (1974). *Type A behavior and your heart.* Knopf.

Grable, J. E. (2000). Financial risk Tolerance and additional factors that affect risk taking in everyday money matters. *Journal of Business and Psychology, 14*(4).

Grable, J. E., & Joo, S. (1999). Factors related to risk tolerance: A further examination. *Consumer Interests Annual, 45*, 53–58.

Grable, J. E., & Lytton, R. H. (1998). Investor risk tolerance: Testing the efficacy of demographics as differentiating and classifying factors. *Journal of Financial Counseling and Planning, 9*(1), 61–74.

Grable, J., & Lytton, R. H. (1999). Financial risk tolerance revisited: The development of a risk assessment instruments. *Financial Services Review, 8*(3), 163–181. https://doi.org/10.1016/s1057-0810(99)00041-4

Grey, R. J., & Gordon, G. G. (1978). Risk-taking managers: Who get the top jobs? *Management Review, 67*, 8–13.

Guiso, L., Haliassos, M., & Jappelli, T. (2003). Household stockholding in Europe: Where do we stand and where do we go? *Economic Policy, 18*(36), 123–170. https://doi.org/10.1111/1468-0327.00104

Guiso, L., & Paiella, M. (2018). Risk aversion, wealth, and background risk. *Journal of the European Economic Association, 6*(6), 1109–1150.

Gutter, M. S., Fox, J. J., & Montalto, C. P. (1999). Racial differences in investor decision making. *Financial Services Review, 8*(3), 149–162.

Hallahan, T. A., Faff, R. W., & McKenzie, M. D. (2004). An empirical investigation of personal financial risk tolerance. *Financial Services Review, 13*(1), 57–78.

Haliassos, M., & Bertaut, C. C. (1995). Why do so few hold stocks? *The Economic Journal, 105*, 1110–1129.

Hanna, S., & Chen, P. (1995). Optimal portfolio: An expected utility/simulation approach. In *Proceedings: Academy of Financial Services*.

Hanna, S., & Chen, P. (1997). Subjective and objective risk tolerance: Implications for optimal portfolios. *Journal of Financial Counseling and Planning, 8*(2), 17–26. https://doi.org/10.2139/ssrn.95488

Hariharan, G., Chapman, K. S., & Domian, D. L. (2000). Risk tolerance and asset allocation for investors nearing retirement. *Financial Services Review, 9*(2), 159–170. https://doi.org/10.1016/S1057-0810(00)00063-9

Hawley, C. B., & Fujii, E. T. (1993). An empirical analysis of preferences for financial risk: Further evidence on the friedman–savage model. *Journal of Post Keynesian Economics, 16*(2), 197–204.

Haynes, S. G., & Matthews, K. A. (1988). The association of Type A behavior with cardiovascular disease-update and critical review. In B. K. Houston & C. R. Snyder (Eds.), *Type A behavior pattern: Research, theory, and intervention* (pp. 51–82). John Wiley & Sons.

Howard, J. H., Cunningham, D. A., & Rechnitzer, P. A. (1977). Work patterns associated with Type A behavior: A managerial population. *Human Relations, 30*, 825–836.

Howells, G. (2005). The potential and limits of consumer empowerment by information. *Journal of Law and Society, 32*(3), 349–370.

Houston, B. K., & Snyder, C. R. (Eds.). (1988). *Type A behavior pattern: Research, theory, and intervention*. John Wiley & Sons.

Huston, S. J. (2010). *Measuring Financial Literacy. 44*(2), 296–316.

Kahneman, D., & Tversky, A. (1979). Prospect theory: An analysis of decision under risk. *Econometrica: Journal of the Econometric Society*, *47*(3), 263–291. https://doi.org/10.1111/j.1536-7150.2011.00774.x

Langrehr, F. W. (1979). Consumer education: Does it change students' competencies and attitudes? *The Journal of Consumer Affairs, 13*, 41–53.

Lazzarone, B. G. (1996). The economic well-being or rural Nevada elders. In *Proceedings of the 1996 Conference of the Western Region Home Management Family Economics Educators,* (pp. 67–74).

Lee, H. K., & Hanna, S. (1991). Wealth and stock ownership. In *Proceedings of the Association for Financial Counseling and Planning Education* (pp. 126–140).

Lee, H. K., & Hanna, S. (1995). Empirical patterns of risk-tolerance. In *Proceedings of the Academy of Financial Services*.

Leonard, D. (1995). Doctor, heal thyself. *Smart Money, 4*, 91–96.

Lovallo, W. R., Pincomb, G. A., Edwards, G. L., Brackett, D. J., & Wilson, M. F. (1986). Work pressure and the Type A behavior pattern exam stress in male medical students. *Psychosomatic Medicine, 48*, 125–133.

Malkiel, B. G. (1996). *A random walk down wall street*. W.W. Norton & Co.

Mandell, L. (1997). Personal financial survey of high school seniors. *Jump Start Coalition for Personal Financial Literacy*, 7.

Mandrik, C. A., & Bao, Y. (2005). *Exploring the concept and measurement of general risk aversion*. ACR North American Advances.

Maslow, A. H. (1954). The instinctoid nature of basic needs. *Journal of Personality, 22*, 326–347. https://doi.org/10.1111/j.1467-6494.1954.tb01136.x

Masters, R. (1989). Study examines investors' risk-taking propensities. *The Journal of Financial Planning, 2*, 151–155.

Masters, R. S. W. (1992). Knowledge, knerves and know-how: the role of explicit versus implicit knowledge in the breakdown of a complex motor skill under pressure. *British Journal of Psychology, 83*, 343–358.

Matthews, K. A., & Siegel, J. M. (1983). Type A behaviors for children, social comparison, and standards for self-evaluation. *Developmental Psychology, 19*(1), 135–140. https://doi.org/10.1037/0012-1649.19.1.135

Mettlin, C. (1976). Occupational careers and the prevention of coronary-prone behavior. *Social Science and Medicine, 10*, 367–372.

Meyer, H. H., Walker, W. B., & Litwin, G. H. (1961). Motive patterns and risk preferences associated with entrepreneurship. *Journal of Abnormal and Social Psychology, 63*, 570–574.

Miller, M., Reichelstein, J., Salas, C., & Zia, B. (2015). Can you help someone become financially capable? A meta-analysis of the literature. *The World Bank Research Observer, 2013*, 1–27. https://doi.org/10.1093/wbro/lkv009

Morin, R.-A., & Suarez, F. (1983). Risk aversion revisited. *The Journal of Finance, 38*, 1201–1216.

Morin, R. A., Fernandez Suarez, A., Brennan, M. J., Ederinifton, L. J., Mehta, D., & Blume, M. (1983). Risk aversion revisited. *The Journal of Finance, 38*(4), 1201–1216.

OECD. (2005). *OECD annual report 2005*. OECD Publishing. https://doi.org/10.1787/annrep-2005-en

Quattlebaum, O. M. (1988). Loss aversion: The key to determining individual risk. *The Journal of Financial Planning, 1*(1), 66–68.

Roszkowski, M. J., Snelbecker, G. E., & Leimberg, S. R. (1993). Risk-tolerance and risk aversion. In S. R. Leimberg, M. J. Satinsky, R. T. LeClair, & R. J. Doyle, Jr. (Eds.), *The tools and techniques of financial planning* (4th ed., pp. 213–225). National Underwriter.

Schooley, D. K., & Worden, D. D. (1996). Risk aversion measures: Comparing attitudes and asset allocation. *Financial Services Review, 5*, 87–99.

Schotter, A., & Trevino, I. (2014). Belief elicitation in the laboratory. *Annual Review of Economics, 6*(1), 103–128.

Shaw, K. L. (1996). An empirical analysis of risk aversion and income growth. *Journal of Labor Economics, 14*, 626–653.

Sorensen, G., Jacobs, D. R., Pirie, P., Folsom, A., Luepker, P., & Gillum, R. (1987). Relationship among Type A behavior, employment experience, and gender: The Minnesota heart survey. *Journal of Behavioral Medicine, 10*, 323–336.

Strube, M. J. (Ed.). (1991). *Type A behavior*. Sage.

Stulz, R. M. (1981). On the effects of barriers to international investment. *The Journal of Finance, 36*(4), 923–934. https://doi.org/10.1111/j.1540-6261.1981.tb04893.x

Subrahmanyam, M. G. (1975). On the optimality of international capital market integration. *Journal of Financial Economics, 2*(1), 3–28. https://doi.org/10.1016/0304-405X(75)90021-5

Sung, J., & Hanna, S. (1996). Factors related to risk tolerance. *Journal of Financial Counseling and Planning, 7*, 11–19. https://doi.org/10.2139/ssrn.2234

Thoresen, C. E., & Low, K. G. (1990). Women and the Type A behavior pattern: Review and commentary. *Journal of Social Behavior and Personality, 6*, 117–133.

Treaty on the European Union. (1992). *Official Journal of the European Union, 35*(C 191), 1–112.

Tversky, A., & Kahneman, D. (1974). Judgment under uncertainty: Heuristics and Biases: Biases in judgments reveal some heuristics of thinking under uncertainty. *Science, 185*(4157), 1124–1131.

Tversky, A., & Kahneman, D. (1992). Advances in prospect-theory—cumulative representation of uncertainty. *Journal of Risk and Uncertainty, 5*(4), 297–323. https://doi.org/10.1007/Bf00122574

Tversky, A., Slovic, P., & Kahneman, D. (1990). The causes of preference reversal. *The American Economic Review*, 204–217.

Updegrave, W. L. (1996, February). *Fund investors need to go back to school, money* (pp. 98–100).

Van Egeren, L. F., Sniderman, L. D., & Roggelin, M. S. (1982). Competitive two-person interactions of Type-A and Type-B individuals. *Journal of Behavioral Medicine, 5*, 55–66.

Wang, H., & Hanna, S. (1997). *Does risk tolerance decrease with age?*

Warner, N., & Cramer, S. (1995). Saving behaviours: First wave baby boomers. *Journal of Consumer Studies & Home Economics, 19*(1), 57–67.

Weidner, G., & Matthews, K. A. (1978). Reported physical symptoms elicited by unpredictable events and the Type A coronary-prone behavior pattern. *Journal of Personality and Social Psychology, 36*, 1213–1220.

Wong, A., & Carducci, B. J. (1991). Sensation seeking and financial risk taking in everyday money matters. *Journal of Business and Psychology, 5*(4), 525–530. https://doi.org/10.1007/BF01014500

Yoo, P. S. (1994). *Age dependent portfolio selection* (Working Papers 1994-003). Federal Reserve Bank of St. Louis.

Zhong, L. X., & Xiao, J. J. (1995). Determinants of family bond and stock holdings. *Financial Counseling and Planning, 6*, 107–114.

Zuckerman, M. (1979). *Beyond the optimal level of arousal.* Lawrence Erlbraum Associates.

Zuckerman, M. (1983). *Sensation seeking and sports*. Personality and individual differences.

Zuckerman, M., Eysenck, S. B., & Eysenck, H. J. (1978). Sensation seeking in England and America: Cross-cultural, age, and sex comparisons. *Journal of Consulting and Clinical Psychology, 46*(1), 139.

CHAPTER 2

Risk Tolerance Tools: From Academia to Regulation and Back

Abstract This chapter takes a closer look at the implementation of the first compliance tool to measure risk tolerance in the European Union—the MiFID suitability questionnaire. The literature review carried out in Chapter 1 has clearly identified the key dimensions of variability that characterized the academic notion of risk tolerance up to the introduction of the suitability questionnaire. This chapter sets out to understand to what degree this notion has helped define the implementation of the suitability requirement in European Regulation ranging from the original requirements proposed in MiFID to the changes introduced with MiFID2 and successive modifications.

Keywords Suitability questionnaire · MiFID · MiFID2 · Risk tolerance tools

© The Author(s), under exclusive license to Springer Nature Switzerland AG 2022
C. Cruciani et al., *Understanding Financial Risk Tolerance*,
https://doi.org/10.1007/978-3-031-13131-8_2

1 The Market in Financial Instruments Directive (MiFID) and its Impact on Risk Tolerance Measurement

1.1 *Introducing MiFID*

1.1.1 A Brief History, Context, and Content

The Market in Financial Instrument Directive (2004/39/EC) represents a turning point for the European financial market and its operators. It entered into force on April 2004 with the obligation for EU countries to incorporate it into national law by 31 January 2007. It amended Council Directives 85/611/EEC and 93/6/EEC and Directive 2000/12/EC of the European Parliament and of the Council and repealed Council Directive 93/22/EEC. It was followed by the "Level-2" Directive (2006/73/EC) and the Commission Regulation 1287/2006/EC, which contain the technical measures to implement operationally what is defined by MiFID.

The Directive responds to the need to create a uniform competitive field («level playing field») between the financial intermediaries of the European Union, without jeopardizing investor protection and the freedom to provide investment services throughout the Community and focuses on investor protection, differentiated according to the degree of financial experience; the integrity of the markets; the strengthening of competition mechanisms, with the abolition of the obligation to concentrate trade on regulated markets; the efficiency of the markets, also aimed at reducing the cost of the services offered; and the improvement of the governance systems of investment firms and better management of conflicts of interest.

Given that the interest of this book is individual risk tolerance, the remainder of this section will provide only a general overview of the contents of MiFID, to dedicate more time to the components that more closely relate to the key goal of the analysis in the following sections.

The Directive requires EU countries to harmonize the rules governing investment services and activities, setting up an authorization system that enables investment firms to register and operate throughout the EU and to offer their services across borders based on the authorization issued by the competent authority of their home country. Being the authorization subject to the same conditions in all EU countries, it promotes the harmonization of rules governing investment firms, benefiting investors, issuers, and other market stakeholders by promoting efficient and competitive markets.

The second building block of the MiFID is prudential assessment, establishing the harmonization of the assessment rules of procedure and criteria for the acquisition of a qualifying holding, i.e., any direct or indirect holding in an investment firm which represents 10% or more of the capital or of the voting rights or which makes it possible to exercise a significant influence over the management of the investment firm in which that holding subsists.

Concerning investor protection, the Directive sets conduct of business rules for providing investment services to clients and minimum standards for the mandate and powers that national competent authorities must have at their disposal. It also establishes effective mechanisms for real-time cooperation in investigating and prosecuting breaches of the rules.

When we move to transparency and market integrity, the directive creates an obligation to safeguard market integrity, to report transactions, and to keep records, introducing a pre-trade transparency obligation. This requires "internalizers" (i.e., firms dealing on their own account by executing client orders outside regulated markets or multilateral trading facilities) to disclose the prices at which they are willing to buy from and/or sell to their clients. However, it limits this disclosure obligation to transactions not above standard market size, defined as the average size of orders executed in the market.

With respect to operator protection, the directive establishes a series of protective measures for "systematic internalizers" when they are obliged to quote prices, so that they can avoid running undesirable risks when they provide this kind of service to clients. These measures include the possibility of updating and withdrawing quoted prices. The directive also establishes a fair market for retail investors. It prevents financial institutions from discriminating those investors, e.g., by offering to some of their improvements to publicly quoted prices.

Finally, the directive establishes that EU countries must appoint their competent authorities and send the necessary information to the Commission, ESMA and the competent authorities of the other EU countries. The competent authorities act as a point of contact in the EU countries and are required to cooperate closely with ESMA, which is in turn in charge of keeping an up-to-date list of these authorities.

1.1.2 Classification of Clients, Disclosure Obligations, Assessment of Appropriateness and Suitability

One of the major novelties introduced by the Market in Financial Instrument Directive (2004/39/EC) is the inclusion of the provision of investment advice among the investment services requiring authorization. This is motivated by the increasing dependence of investors on personal recommendations and, at the same time, by the necessity to protect them.

MiFID requires investment firms to classify their clients in order to modulate the information obligations to be fulfilled and the safeguards to be guaranteed.

Clients are divided into three categories: retail clients, defined as residual category and including individuals who are neither professional clients nor qualifying counterparties; professional clients,[1] i.e., all entities authorized to carry out investment services, national and local governments, public entities, central banks and international institutions, private-law companies exceeding certain turnover limits; and qualifying counterparties,[2] i.e., a subset of professional clients consisting of investment firms, credit and insurance institutions, pension funds, national governments, central banks, and international institutions.

The classifycation of clients is functional to the identification of the informative obligations to be carried out. In general, however, regardless of the category, clients have the right to receive sufficient information to make informed and honest, clear and not misleading investment choices. Areas of disclosure for all client categories include their assigned classification, any conflicts of interest, any commissions paid to third parties, a description of the securities, the execution policy and information on losses.

In addition, intermediaries must communicate their policies and measures for the protection of clients, their own assessment of the client's portfolio instruments, and the costs associated with the services provided.

From the point of view of client protection, MiFID does not limit itself to providing intermediaries with information obligations but requires them to carry out tests on the nature of the investment service offered or requested by the client. An appropriateness test shall be carried out in

[1] A retail client may apply to be considered professional, after undergoing a suitability assessment by the investment firm.

[2] Access to this category is not automatic since the client must confirm his/her will to be treated as an eligible counterparty.

the case of provision of the financial advisory service. The intermediary must verify that the advice provided corresponds to the investment objectives of the client to whom it is addressed and that it is appropriate to his assets. It is up to the intermediary to collect all the information necessary to understand whether the knowledge and experience of the client is sufficient for a correct evaluation of the advice provided.

The suitability test is provided, instead, for all other Investment services. In this case, the criteria are the information and experiences that the client has about the specific financial product and the general level of financial culture. A particular case is the execution-only mode, in which it is not necessary to carry out the appropriateness test and there are no informative obligations apart from the moment in which the client accesses this type of service. The execution-only mode can be chosen only for not complex financial instruments and must be expressly requested by the client. If this is the case, the investment firm shall specify that it will not carry out the appropriateness test. The purpose of execution-only mode is to reduce time and costs. Given the relevance of the concept of risk tolerance for the suitability questionnaire the next sections will be dedicated to its structure and empirical validity.

1.2 MiFID and the Suitability Questionnaire

1.2.1 Questionnaire Overview

The introduction of MiFID contributed to bring about several important modifications to the financial services landscape, with the introduction of a suitability questionnaire being one of the most relevant to operationalize risk tolerance. Filling out this questionnaire becomes a mandatory activity to protect clients' interests by identifying financial needs and preferences, but also to protect financial firms from complaints in case of losses.

A first element to consider is which information is required to be collected by investment firms when providing financial advice and portfolio management. MiFID's Article 19 point 4 mentions that financial knowledge, experience with a particular product, financial situation, and investment objective need to be properly evaluated by investment firms to ensure that the firm's recommendations are suitable for the client, with Member States overseeing the process to ensure that the service or product is appropriate (Art. 19, point 5). The MiFID Implementing Directive, also called Level-2 Directive spells out the specific information that needs to be collected by investment firms to assess suitability

(Commission of the European Communities, 2006). In particular, Article 35 presents the three criteria that must be met when providing an investment recommendation: the investment objective of the client must be met; the client can bear the financial risk involved with the pursuit of that investment objective; the client has the necessary knowledge to understand the financial risk involved. Points 3 and 4 of the same article discuss what is actually included in the information regarding financial situation, namely "information on the source and extent of his regular income, his assets, including liquid assets, investments and real property, and his regular financial commitments" (Art. 35, point 3) and regarding the investment objectives, namely "information on the length of time for which the client wishes to hold the investment, his preferences regarding risk-taking, his risk profile, and the purposes of the investment" (Art. 35, point 4). We need to turn to Article 37 to find out more about what is meant by information regarding experience and knowledge which must include "types of service, transaction and financial instrument with which the client is familiar; nature, volume, and frequency of the clien''s transactions in financial instruments and the period over which they have been carried out; level of education, and profession or relevant former profession of the client or potential client" (Art. 37, point 1).

The European Securities and Market Authority (ESMA) was called to provide clarification regarding the implementation of the suitability requirements and produced a series of guidelines regarding the exact information that should be collected (ESMA, 2012). The list includes for example the marital status, the family situation (with regard as to how they might evolve over time), the employment situation (focusing on the position in the life cycle that the client is currently living in), and the need for liquidity (general guideline 2, supporting guideline 22). The Guidelines also elaborate on the principle of proportionality in information collection introduced in MiFID: the extent of the data collection depends on the complexity of the financial product being recommended or purchased; complex products will require to collect all the necessary information including regular and total income, all clients assets, including deposition, pensions funds and personal and investment property and all regular financial commitments, implying that the debt position should also be known (general guideline 4, supporting guideline 34). The nature of the service requested should drive the information collection, with clients looking for financial advice over the entire portfolio providing more information than clients looking for a specific advice (supporting guideline 36). The potentially vulnerable nature of the client should also drive information collection, especially concerning age and financial vulnerability (supporting guideline 37). Regarding the reliability of the information collected, the guidelines suggest counterbalancing clients' self-assessed information with objective criteria, working on the questions' wording and concepts: for instance, instead of directly asking if a client has enough funds to invest, one can ask about the current financial situation and make an inference on the client's liquidity.

It is noteworthy that some of the drivers that had already been identified in the literature regarding financial risk tolerance are not included in the MiFID requirements: among them, some like age, gender, and marital status are very easily available to a financial advisor filling out a suitability questionnaire and have been found to be very important for the analysis of risk preferences.

1.2.2 Implementing the Directive: Empirical Evidence and Practitioners' Views

The description of the requirements set forth in the MiFID Directive and in the Implementing Directive have been only slightly clarified in the Guidelines, leaving significant wiggle room to define several key concepts. Several authors highlight this as the key concern in the development of the suitability questionnaire, especially for the impact on risk tolerance.

Early literature stresses that suitability questionnaires miss out on the opportunity to really measure risk-relevant dimensions. De Palma and Picard (2010) report the first study explicitly addressing the effectiveness of the suitability questionnaires developed by 10 French financial intermediaries including banks and wealth advisors in the three years since the entry into force of MiFID. The analysis focuses on the questionnaire content with respect to the requirements of the Directive and on the ability of the questionnaires to properly measure what they set out to measure: risk-taking preferences. The paper identifies three dimensions of such preferences that are deemed necessary to provide investment advice: risk tolerance, loss tolerance, and the tendency to distort probabilities, but finds that only the first element is properly addressed in the questionnaires. Moreover, only one-third of the questionnaires provides a quantitative measure of risk aversion, despite most try to provide some form of measurement. The lack of a uniform, quantitative way of measuring risk aversion prevents questionnaires from defining a homogeneous type of advice for clients with the same characteristics and investment plan across different institutions. The authors conclude that the use of too abstract questions and the excessive reliance on subjective evaluations prevent from developing sound measures of risk aversion to use for devising appropriate financial advice: only 2 out of 10 questionnaires can reach a minimum explanatory power in terms of risk aversion.[3]

Marinelli and Mazzoli (2011) start from considering that the lack of precise indication regarding the content of suitability questionnaires is likely to have produced very different templates in different institutions and run a similar analysis on a sample of 14 Italian questionnaires covering 90% of the Italian market. In a descriptive analysis of the 14 questionnaires the paper shows very important differences starting from the question number, ranging from 9 to 37 questions. Only one questionnaire covers all the areas mentioned in the Directives, most focus on investment horizon, risk-taking preferences, type of service, experience of the client with respect to the product and with financial instruments but neglect regular financial commitments, asset composition, risk profile and the duration of past investments. If French questionnaire were accused to be too reliant in subjective and abstract evaluations, the Italian experience shows a narrow focus on objective risk without considering any subjective attitude to a general situation of riskiness. The paper also includes an interesting comparison of the implications of using different questionnaires: 100 subjects received and filled out three further questionnaires and the way in which they are classified[4]is compared, showing that in 77% of the cases the classification received is different across the three institutions.

Linciano and Soccorso (2012) extend the work of Marinelli and Mazzoli using a sample of 20 questionnaires collected from Italian financial institutions focusing also on the process set in place by them to devise this suitability tool. The survey shows that most of the institutions developed the questionnaire in house, without the help of specific experts and, despite declaring to have validated the tool, most did not run a

[3] The authors develop a Risk index based on items required by MiFID and use clients' information to compute a risk score and compare it with the scores attributed by the suitability questionnaires. The minimum explanatory power is set at 40%—questions in the suitability questionnaires explain 40% of the variability in the risk index for the population.

[4] The three banks had different classification schemes for clients that were harmonized in a single scale to allow for proper comparisons.

pilot study. Only 3 out of 20 institutions have different questionnaires for different clients (natural and legal persons), most institutions provide training to the personnel in charge of administering the questionnaire, but the training is not specific to the questionnaire but rather pertinent to the new regulatory requirements. Moving to the questionnaires' content, the suitability tools were largely in line with the requirements: all include three sections, one for each for the key domains identified by MiFID (experience and knowledge, financial situation, investment objectives) with varying numbers of questions. Some include a socio-demographic section (not explicitly required by MiFID) but only 4 questionnaires ask about the client's age or marital status and the question on family composition is almost always absent. Regarding knowledge and experience, the authors remark how none of the questionnaires mentions "positive risk-return trade-off" and only one mentions risk diversification; the only dimension of knowledge that is ascertained deals with investment products not with relevant investment concepts. Regarding financial situation most questionnaires focus on regular financial commitment and only 4 also ask if the client has insurance policies or retirement plans. The section on investment objectives is the least detailed, despite being the one where two important dimensions of risk are included: risk preferences (objective risk) and risk profile (subjective risk). Only 13 out of 20 questionnaires have at least one question on objective risk and only 10 on subjective risk. The authors conclude that most of the suitability questionnaires analyzed provide "an ambiguous definition of risk" (ibid, page 35) since the assessment of risk preferences is mixed with considerations on investment horizon and goals. Moreover, investors are not asked to react to specific scenarios but rather to state the preferred level of risk or investment purpose. Only 2 out of the 20 questionnaires included in the study are deemed "clear, effective and valid" (ibid, page 35).

Mazzoli and Marinelli (2014) continue the exploration of Italian suitability questionnaires checking its content against the findings of the determinants of financial investment derived from a sample of Italian household from the Bank of Italy Survey of Household Income and Wealth held in 2008. The Survey includes some questions regarding financial risk tolerance (three different measures, one objective, one subjective, and a situational one) that are used to select 1149 head of households that display consistent risk attitudes across all of them. Using the other information included in the survey, the authors determine which features are important for the decision of whether to invest in risky assets and which ones are important to determine how much to invest. The likelihood to invest is positively affected by financial literacy, being married or employed, owning a house or having a positive general economic situation and older age, while gender does not lead to significant results. The decision regarding how much to invest in risky assets is influenced by very different variables: it negatively depends on having other financial debt, it positively depends on income and is not affected by the number of economic dependencies or the net amount of wealth. All these relationships offer a map to navigate the potential dimensions of financial risk tolerance that might be picked up in suitability questionnaires, but the analysis of 25 such tools from Italian banks shows that there is a significant misalignment between what should be included and what actually is: for what concerns the determinants of the decision to invest in risky assets, only 16% of the questionnaires ask about house ownership, none asks about age, 12% ask about being married and 48% ask about employment status. When it comes to the determinants of how much to invest, only 40% explore the details regarding regular income and only 36% ask about outstanding financial commitments other than mortgages. Questionnaires focus very narrowly on risk attitudes but seem to want to ask clients to state their desired level of risk given the investment objective rather than focusing on its determinants.

Overall, these studies highlight that the implementation of the suitability requirement in MiFID was not at all a smooth process and that a smoother connection between academic knowledge and practical implications was still lacking.

Taking on the perspective of financial advisors, Valiante and Assi (2011) present the results of a survey conducted by the European Capital Markets Institute aimed at providing a qualitative description of the state of implementation and appraisal of MiFID among different regulatory authorities and financial institutions. The survey involved 43 different entities, with investment firms representing 37% of the final sample of respondents. The general impression about the introduction of MiFID shows that respondents are in general positive about the changes brought about by the new Directive, in particular for the reduction in trading fee and the positive effect on investment in technologies and infrastructures, although concerns are raised about quality of some trading data necessary for transparency purposed and for the implementation costs of all MiFID requirements. Regarding suitability, all respondents appear to have in place an effective system, although investment firms are the only ones keeping suitability carefully updated.

Hübner and Plunus (2013) suggest that the suitability requirements did not meet the favors of practitioners as they did not even clearly define what it meant by risk profile, let alone providing suggestions for the key areas to address that "looked way too much like the administrative translation of what financial advisors were already doing" (ibid, page 2).

2 The Academic Debate After MiFID

Chapter 1 provided a short history of the relevance of understanding financial risk tolerance both from an academic and a market point of view. On one side, new investment opportunities became relevant and necessary due to societal and regulatory changes even beyond the boundaries of financial markets, making investment firms and advisors key players in the transition and requiring to start regulating markets more carefully. On the other side, financial risk tolerance easily became a new testing ground for expressing the long-term fascination economics had for risk attitudes, ranging from traditional investigations (regarding demographic factors) to more dynamic version of this concept (e.g. the relevance of life events).

The previous section discussed how the introduction of MiFID as key response to this need to rationalize new financial opportunities and balance need for investor protection with need for diffusion of financial services did not seem to exploit the findings from academic research, in part due to the unclear suggestion provided in the formal regulation. This section updates the academic debate by looking at the factors already identified in Chapter 1 and providing updates on relevant findings that support or improve upon the current knowledge. The goal of this review defines the publication time frame (2005–2014) that is being analyzed, as 2014 marks the publication of the new version of MiFID, the Markets in Financial Instruments 2. Will the regulators have taken better stock of the available empirical findings this time around?

The next section provides the information that will be necessary to answer this question. Given that the key features of many empirical analyses have been presented in Chapter 1, this review will be selective and detail only the novel findings, while Table 1 will classify all the new publications broadly confirming what had been established in Chapter 1 regarding the relationship between specific variables and risk tolerance.

Table 1 Factors influencing financial risk tolerance—an academic view before MiFID2 (2005–2014)

Variable	*Effect on risk tolerance*	*References*
Age	Older individuals are less risk tolerant	Hammitt et al. (2009), Dohmen et al. (2011), Sahm (2012) and Bogan and Fertig (2013)
	Older individuals are more risk tolerant	Hammitt et al. (2009), Bateman et al. (2011) and Bateman et al. (2012)
Gender	Males are more risk tolerant than females	Yao and Hanna (2005), Lyons et al. (2008), Neelakantan (2010) and Sahm (2012)
	Male overestimate their risk tolerance while females underestimate it	Grable and Roszkowski (2007)
Education and financial literacy	More educated individuals are more risk tolerant	van Rooij et al. (2011) and Sahm (2012)
Marital status and economic dependencies	Being married reduces risk tolerance for both gender but more so for females	Yao and Hanna (2005) and Sahm (2012)
	Being married increases risk tolerance for both gender	Bertocchi et al. (2011)
Income and wealth	Wealthier individuals are more risk tolerant	Bateman et al. (2011) and Grable et al. (2006)
	Wealth/income changes do not significantly affect risk tolerance of individuals	Brunnermeier and Nagel (2008) and Sahm (2012)
Life events	Job displacement or being diagnosed with a serious health condition do not permanently affect risk aversion	Sahm (2012)
	Mixed results regarding the effect of natural events	Cameron (2010) and Page et al. (2014)
Behavioral and personality factors	Individualism increases risk tolerance	Breuer et al. (2014) and Grable and Roszkowski (2008)
	Being in a good mood increases risk tolerance	

2.1 *Socio-Demographic Variables*

Regarding **age**, the results remain mixed. This is not surprising as time diversification can work both ways: younger individuals have more time to recover from potential losses and may more light-heartedly engage in riskier behavior while at the same time smoothing consumption over a longer horizon. This time diversification allows younger individuals to be more risk tolerant and risk tolerance to decrease over time. On the other hand, younger individuals face the consequences of a bad financial choice over a longer time horizon, thus being reluctant to engage in risk behavior. This diversification effect would make older individuals more risk tolerant (Hammitt et al., 2009).

Bateman et al. (2011) use two choice experiments involving over 800 individuals right before and after the financial crisis of 2007 to address the impact of the crisis on risk aversion in combination with socio-demographic factors and find that older and wealthier individuals continue to exhibit riskier choices both before and after the financial crisis. The fact that older age is associated with higher risk tolerance is also found in Bateman et al. (2012).

The opposite pattern is found in Dohmen et al. (2011), who use a representative sample of the German population[5] and different measure of risk tolerance (a self-assessed, subjective measure and real-stakes lottery experiments) and find that risk tolerance decreases steadily with age for men, while it decreases more markedly until 30 years old for women and then it remains relatively flat, both for women who have children and for those who do not.

It is interesting to consider that age might interact with other age-related variables, such as health; in fact, health concerns become greater as individuals age and may induce individuals to hold more liquid and safe assets: Bogan and Fertig (2013) look at cognitive limitations and psychiatric problems using data from six different waves of the Health and Retirement Survey and show that household where such issues exist tend to invest up to 19% fewer resources in risky assets.

Regarding **gender,** the literature confirms the results highlighted in Chapter 1 showing that females tend to be less risk tolerant than males.

[5] They use the German Socio-Economic Panel (SOEP), a representative sample of more than 22,000 individuals.

An interesting research shows that males tend to overestimate their financial risk tolerance significantly while females tend to underestimate it (Grable and Roszkowski, 2007). Using a sample of 1751 individuals involved in an online survey between 2002 and 2003 and assessing subjective self-perception of risk tolerance[6] in comparison with a more complex measure of risk tolerance (the Grable-Lytton risk tolerance scale) the authors show that, even controlling for other factors such as income or age, females are more likely to underestimate their risk tolerance, even if the effect is small, but statistically significant. This paper is particularly interesting because it attempts to shed light on the reasons why women are so often found to be less risk tolerant looking at subjective factors that are often overlooked but likely to have a great impact.

Regarding **education and financial literacy**, the literature shows that both are positively correlated with risk tolerance and stock-market participation. For instance, van Rooij et al. (2011) use a representative sample of the Dutch population to show that financial literacy positively explains stock-market participation.

Regarding **marital status and economic dependencies**, Bertocchi et al. (2011) find that being married is a source of financial security and makes married individuals more financially risk tolerant.

Yao and Hanna (2005) use several waves of the Survey of Consumer Finance employing a subjective, self-assessed measure of risk tolerance and show that being married somewhat mitigates risk tolerance in males, as unmarried men are more risk tolerant than married men, but both categories are more risk tolerant than unmarried and married women.

Regarding **income and wealth**, Brunnermeier and Nagel (2008) use data from a longitudinal study tracking families over time to explore how variations in wealth are reflected in risk aversion. The data show that changes in liquid wealth positively affect stock-market participation, but wealth changes are not positively correlated with investing in riskier assets—market entry but not individual-specific risk aversion is affected by increases in liquid wealth. This pattern is partially explained by inertia in portfolio rebalancing.

[6] Individuals were asked the following question: "In general, how would your best friend describe you as a risk taker?" and had to choose among the following options: a real gambler, willing to take risks after completing adequate research, cautious, and a real risk avoider.

Sahm (2012) also shows that income and wealth changes do not significantly affect financial risk tolerance using the hypothetical gamble question of several waves of the Health and Retirement Study. This paper also looks at the implications of several socio-demographic variables, whose results are summarized in Table 1.

2.2 *Life Events*

The literature on life events is more sparse, as many different events might be considered. Sahm (2012) looks at job displacement or the diagnosis of a serious illness and shows that neither produces long-term changes to financial risk tolerance. Similarly, while individuals' risk tolerance is significantly influenced by macroeconomic trends (increases in the Index of Consumer Sentiment map onto an increase in risk tolerance) the effect is not persistent but fades away within a year.

Roszkowski and Davey (2010) find that risk tolerance is not significantly affected after the global financial crisis and the only risk perceptions are changed.

When it comes to natural disasters, Cameron (2010) discusses how having been subject to a flood or a earthquake decreases risk tolerance, while Page et al. (2014) show that homeowners affects by large losses after a natural disaster in Australia behave consistently with prospect theory and exhibit more risk seeking behavior than individuals with similar characteristics (including home value).

2.3 *Behavioral and Personality Factors*

Grable et al. (2006) use a survey with 1355 adults to address if risk tolerance responds to changes in price in the US Stock exchange to discuss the role of projection bias and vividness. Showing that only recent price changes affect the level of risk tolerance predicted with the Grable-Lytton 13-item scale, the authors discuss how individuals are prone to representativeness in projecting recent past performance into expected performance and are more strongly affected by events that are salient and easy to recall, consistently with the bias of availability or vividness.

Mayfield et al. (2008) focus on the role of personality traits and show that different traits are linked to the preference for long-term investment (openness to experiences) or short-term investment (extraversion).

Breuer et al. (2014) use survey data collected on a sample of university students in Germany and Singapore including socio-demographic, attitudinal, and risk questions and find that the subjective assessment of one's attitude to risk is significantly positively explained by individualism, even when controlling for socio-demographic and attitudinal questions.

2.4 Risk Tolerance: Stable Trait or Adaptive Feature?

Several of the articles reviewed in the previous sections have shown that financial risk tolerance seems to vary more across fixed features such as age or gender than across transient events like a job loss. Sahm (2012) estimates that 73% in the variability she observed is due entirely to socio-demographic factors—age, gender, race, and education—and she concludes that most of the systematic differences in risk tolerance are due to "characteristics, such as gender and ethnicity, that are constant over time for a particular individual" (ibid, p. 17). Even macroeconomic conditions in her sample have but a temporary effect on risk tolerance.

Anderson and Mellor (2009) challenge further the idea of stability, showing that risk tolerance seems to vary even across different elicitation methods: they use real-stake economic experiments and hypothetical gambles in a within-subject design and show that for most individuals the two measures are not significantly associated.

As shown in the previous section, Grable et al. (2006) have shown that behavioral factors are likely to shape risk tolerance, but that this effect lingers only over short time intervals.

Van de Venter et al. (2012) use a proprietary psychometric financial risk assessment test to investigate the stability of risk preferences over time (between 2002 and 2006) in Australia: 372 individuals completed more than one survey including financial risk tolerance, socio-economic and attitudinal questions over 5 years. Results show that financial risk tolerance varies minimally and in coherence with a normal distribution, with only an increase in the number of dependencies increasing it slightly. The authors conclude that risk tolerance "is a genetic and predispositional stable personality trait and as such is highly unlikely to fluctuate over the life of an individual" (ibid, p. 7).

3 The Market in Financial Instruments Directive 2 (MiFID2)

3.1 *MiFID2, Context and Content*

Introduced in May 2014 and entered into force on January 3, 2018, the Markets in Financial Instruments Directive 2, or MiFID2 (European Parliament and Council of the European Union, 2014a) alongside the Markets in Financial Instruments Regulation or MiFIR (European Parliament and Council of the European Union, 2014b), provide new ground rules for financial markets in the European Union in the aftermath of the financial crisis. The stated objectives of MiFID2 are bold and encompass a strengthened view on investor protection implemented through increased responsibilities of financial actors and supervisory authorities.

While MiFID2 is more focused on market regulation and organization, MiFIR focuses more on trade transparency data and on derivatives trading and the supervisory rules, with the stated goal to "establish uniform rules applicable in all Member States" (Premise 3, MiFIR).

MiFID2 puts investor protection at its core and introduces a series of measures targeted at providing this all-around protection. Since the focus of this book is how financial risk tolerance and its measurement impact financial advice provision, this overview will be more focused on the features of MiFID2 that relate to this goal. The importance of financial advice as a financial service had been sanctioned already in MiFID with the introduction in the list of investment services and activities (Annex I, Section A) but is reinforced in MiFID2 in the Preamble (p. 12) where the increased relevance of this service is used as a motivation for strengthening conduct of business obligations to ensure investor protection.

The Directive reinforces the concept of transparency and provides for it to be present at all stages of the involvement of individuals in financial markets: this implies transparency on fees, costs for financial advice and timing of information provision (Article 24(4)), with the notable introduction of the formal distinction between independent and non-independent financial advisory spelled out clearly in Article 24(7). Moreover, the Directive aims at reorganizing the supply of financial products by introducing two types of safeguards that apply before and after a financial product is created. The creation of a new financial product is in fact subject to the so-called **product governance**, according to which each financial product needs to have a positive and a negative target market when it is presented to the market: the positive target market identifies the clientele for which the product is more suitable, while the negative target market determines the categories of clients to whom the product cannot be placed. Once developed and marketed for sale in the European Union, financial products are also subject to **product intervention** by the regulatory authorities[7] according to MiFIR and can prohibit or restrict the marketing distribution or sales of financial products.

While product governance seems more strictly related to financial products, the identification of the positive and negative target markets shows how important client classification via suitability questionnaires is crucial as it may end up preventing individuals from having access to some types of investment. The next section will detail precisely how MiFID2 proposes to improve on suitability assessment compared to MiFID.

3.2 Suitability and MiFID2

MiFID2 introduces new content and more formal definitions of the information that needs to be collected by advisors to determine the client profile in terms of suitability and to devise the investment recommendation. Article 25 defines that suitability need not extend only to the clients' dimension, but that "natural persons giving investment advice or information about financial instruments, investment services or ancillary services to clients on behalf of the investment firm possess the necessary knowledge and competence to fulfil their obligations" (ibid, p. 60) including the suitability consideration to the advisors as well. The European Securities and Markets Authority (ESMA) is set in charge to provide guidelines on how to assess advisors' knowledge and competence.

The same article identifies the principle that the financial recommendation should be suitable for two dimensions of the clients' profiles: risk tolerance and the ability to bear losses. Thus, the Directive expands the three domains of suitability already introduced with MiFID: knowledge and experience now apply also to the advisor, the financial situation requires to consider explicitly the ability to bear losses and the investment

[7] Authorities with product-intervention power are the three European Supervisory Authorities (ESMA, EBA and EIOPA) and the National Competent Authorities. At the time of writing, ESMA had two product intervention measures in effect.

objectives must be defined in relation to the client's risk tolerance. Suitability needs also to be clearly explained to the client in relation to the client's characteristics (Art. 25, point 6).

While the idea of risk tolerance is not new to suitability requirements, the ability to bear losses certainly is. Nevertheless, the phrase appears only twice in the MiFID2 and no further clarifications are given in the Directive. ESMA launched a consultation with stakeholders in 2018 and in November published a new set of guidelines for investment advice and portfolio management, highlighting some interesting dimensions of the possible content of suitability questionnaires compliant with MiFID2 (ESMA, 2018). Under the header "Know your client and know your product" ESMA listed a series of important suggestions to devise effective questionnaires including paying attention to the structure of the questionnaire and not only to the content, as layout, font size, order, and type of questions all have an impact in the way in which individuals provide answers. Moreover, overcoming a weakness that was also exposed in an earlier sec "ion of" this chapter, attention should be given to ensuring that clients have knowledge about financial concepts like the risk-return trade-off and not just products. Suggestion 27 lists some of the variables that might be collected to ascertain financial situations and investment objective, including marital status, family situation (especially with respect to changes), age, employment situation, and need for liquidity for a specific purpose. More generally, point 28 suggests looking beyond purely economic information to preferences for environment, social, and governance factors.

3.3 Implementing the Directive: Empirical Evidence and Practitioners' Views

The literature exploring practioners' perception about MiFID2 implementation and potential challenges is currently limited, especially concerning empirical analyses.

Loonen (2020) surveys a representative sample of 267 Dutch investment advisors to understand their perceptions regarding how MiFID2 has impacted their work since its entry into force. Most advisors consider that their job has become more demanding, especially if they work for a medium-size investment firm; advisors with more seniority tend to also report that their job has become less enjoyable. Although 57.9% of respondents indicate that the MiFID2 requirements are clear, 77.4%

indicate that there is a lot of internal discussion regarding implementation. Being male or working for a small- or medium-sized firm implies being more critical regarding effectiveness, while seniority leads to experiencing more debate about MiFID2 implementation and effectiveness. Interestingly, advisors who believe that MiFID helps in providing better advice attribute to cost transparency the bulk of the responsibility for it and 46% of respondents are neutral with respect to the introduction of the requirement to measure the ability to bear losses in terms of whether it contributes to improving investor protection.

Huettinger and Krašauskaitė (2020) focus on the implications of MiFID2 on the investment industry in the Baltic States conducting 9 in-depth interviews with professionals with 5-year work experience in Baltic banks and a degree in economics. The results show that MiFID2 will lead to significant implementation costs, especially for medium-size entities that might work as a barrier to the entry of new players, leading to a possible consolidation in the Baltic market. Respondents call attention upon the possible unintended effects due to the fact that some proposals risk to be too restrictive: for instance, product governance might end up restricting investors' choice and lead financial firms to implement different strategies with small retail clients, who will then end up with fewer, lower-quality choices.

Loonen and Janssen (2022) explore how European private banks are complying with the MiFID2 requirements, addressing how the know-your-customer prescriptions are applied in practice and how compliance with investor protection requirements is implemented. The authors conducted 25 semi-structured interviews with managers and policymakers working for private banks located in Western and Southern Europe with at least five years of seniority on the job. The results show that the 25 institutions use very different formats for the suitability questionnaire, ranging from 15 to 49 questions; 44% update annually the information collected, while 26% do so only every 3–5 years and the rest has different updating rules according to the client's risk profile. Despite the relevance attributed by the regulation to ensuring that questionnaire formats are structured effectively, only 40% of respondents use a variety of different questions avoiding repetitive structures. Moreover, knowledge and experience are more likely assessed once and not more frequently over the life of the relationship for 30% of the sample and 56% (52%) consider that previous professions (education) are not relevant (although are included). The determination of the financial position appears to be more in line with the ESMA guidelines: income and assets versus liabilities are requested, although expenses are not always present. Interestingly 40% of private banks do not collect and process information regarding the client's relationship with other banks. Regarding investment objective, some banks allow for more than one objective to be pursued at once, with only 48% allowing one objective per account. The pursuit of objectives is monitored annually by most. Despite being made clear in MiFID2 as well, only 36% of respondents include the difference between risk willingness with respect to a given investment goal and risk attitude, which is a more general attitude toward risk and is irrespective of amounts and investment products. Regarding the ability to bear losses only 44% of respondents have a quantitative process to determine it, but most focus just on the portfolio and only some on the client's total assets. This new requirement introduced by MiFID2 seems to be the dimension in which banks seem to require more clarifications in terms of the required implementation. The authors conclude that there seems to be a different understanding of key concepts such as risk willingness, ability to bear losses and risk attitude, which naturally map into different procedural practices but need to be harmonized to ensure a uniform investor protection.

Introduced as a response to the trust crisis sweeping over financial markets after the financial crisis, MiFID2 introduced several new requirements and reshaped the way in which investor protection is formulated in the European Union. On one hand, some of the shortcomings related to the MiFID suitability questionnaire seem to have been addressed, such as the need for better definition of the informational requirements or a clearer accent toward knowledge of financial concepts as opposed to products. The evidence presented though has shown that not all market players are facing the challenge in the same way, given that some concepts remain blurry and allow for different interpretations. On the other hand, the new Directive introduces novel restrictions and new requirements that increase disclosure content and costs. Moreover, despite addressing the concept that the ability to bear losses might be a separate dimension to evaluate, indirectly building on behavioral findings regarding the different risk implications regarding losses and gains, the Directive implies a periodic and thorough flow of information that might trigger behavioral responses in terms of cognitive overload that the Directive is not currently addressing.

4 The Academic Debate After MiFID2

This section looks at the evolution of the academic debate on risk tolerance after the publication of the MiFID2 and focuses on a time interval starting with 2015 up until today. As in a previous similar section, the literature review is selective and organized around the key areas identified above and in Chapter 1. Novel findings are discussed more in detail, while papers that broadly confirm previous findings are directly summarized in Table 2, which summarizes all findings and highlights the key effects on risk tolerance.

4.1 Socio-Demographic Factors

Looking at interaction among **age** and different variables provides a series of interesting insights into the true relationship between age and risk aversion. In particular, Blanchett et al. (2018) find that older individuals display risk preferences that are not independent from equity values. The study explores how wealth affects the share of risky assets that individuals hold across life. The paper uses a measure of risk aversion based on three survey questions[8] and looks at individuals involved in defined-contribution plans offered by Morningstar Associates over a 6-year time frame (2006–2012) and finds that older investors' preferences are better represented by DARA preferences,[9] showing that equity values and age interact: if older investors are assessed when the equity values are low they tend to be more risk averse and prefer certain assets over riskier ones, while they would do the opposite when assessed in times of higher equity values.

Another study that brings a step forward the relationship between age and risk tolerance posits that cognition rather than age can help determine a change in risk aversion as individuals age. According to Bonsang

[8] All questions regard expectations regarding retirement investment; the first asks in general, the second question ask about expectations in a bear market and the third about expectations over the next two years.

[9] The paper uses the difference between Constant Relative Risk Aversion preferences (CARA) and Decreasing Relative Risk Aversion preferences (DARA). With CARA preferences, risk aversion is independent from wealth and individuals should hold the same fraction of risky assets across life despite changes in wealth. With DARA risk aversion depends on wealth, as individuals like to hold more (fewer) risky assets when they get wealthier (poorer).

Table 2 Factors influencing financial risk tolerance—an academic view before MiFID2 (2015-now)

Variable	*Effect*	*References*
Age	Negative relationship, especially up to middle age, not necessarily linear	Schurer (2015), Mata et al. (2016), Dohmen et al. (2017), Falk et al. (2018), Banks et al. (2020), and Lippi and Rossi (2020)
Gender	Males are more risk tolerant than females	Falk et al. (2018)
	Perceptions about own abilities and attitudes matters in explaining female lower risk tolerance	Montford and Goldsmith (2016) and Marinelli et al. (2017)
Education and financial literacy	Positive relationship	Kannadhasan (2015), Outreville (2015), Huang et al. (2016), Bannier and Neubert (2016), and Chiang and Xiao (2017)
Marital status and economic dependencies	Interaction between husband and wife determine final risk allocation	Brooks et al. (2019)
	Marriage reduces risk tolerance and separating increases it	Browne et al. (2016b)
Health	Positive relationship	Hammitt et al. (2009)
Life events	Life events impact significantly risk preferences, but that their effect fades over time	Chiang and Xiao (2017) and Kettlewell (2019)
Behavioral factors	Personality traits, sensation seeking and locus of control matter in determining risk tolerance	Wong and Carducci (2016), Fisher and Yao (2017), Kesavayuth et al. (2018), and De Bortoli et al. (2019)

and Dohmen (2015) cognition is correlated with age but not entirely determined by the passing of time; other factors like better schooling, better health care, and life conditions determine lower cognitive levels in populations that enjoy them rather than in less affluent societies. Cognition mediated by age explains the changes in risk aversion and not age itself. Using the first and second SHARE survey[10] waves in 2004 and 2006, they show that older individuals are more risk averse than younger ones and that all cognitive tests decline with age. Regression analyses show that age differences in risk aversion are statistically significant, but once cognition, socio-demographic characteristics, and corrections for possible measurement errors in cognition are included, the age coefficient becomes insignificant in explaining risk aversion.

Using a self-reported measure of math skills Falk et al. (2018) show that risk aversion tends to be more present in individuals with lower cognitive abilities and this holds true in the large majority (over 75%) of the 76 world countries involved in the study in 2012. There is significant evidence of the positive relationship between cognition and risk tolerance in empirical literature.

Regarding **gender**, besides several papers continuing to document the tendency of women to be less risk tolerant than men, we observe an increase in papers trying to provide an explanation for this pattern.

Brooks et al. (2019) explore a large sample of real investors to assess gender differences in risk aversion and measure whether they can be attributed to factors like age, financial experience, wealth, marital status, and employment levels. The study relies on a database of real-life interactions between 4000 independent financial advisors and their male and female clients provided by financial planning solutions based in the United Kingdom, Distribution Technology (DT) using over 500,000 completed questionnaires from 2011 to 2016. The results suggest that women are more risk averse than men, risk tolerance changes significantly with age to then decrease for both genders. The decrease in risk tolerance is faster for men than women; nevertheless, men remain significantly more risk tolerant at all ages. Individuals declaring to have a higher ability to bear losses are also more risk tolerant, but this is truer for men than for women on average. Even controlling for the level of responsibility in one's profession, gender differences persist and are even stronger for high-responsibility job, where men are even more risk tolerant than women in the same positions. The effect of gender declines once investment experience is controlled for. Moreover, there is a positive relationship between risk tolerance and experience for both men and women, but the effect of increased experience increases risk tolerance more for men.

[10] The Survey periodically interviews around 30,000 European individuals.

Besides looking at socio-economic factors there are two other main strands of explanations for this gender divide in risk preference patterns: the first one is rooted in biological differences between males and females and focuses on the role of hormones and genetic differences; the second explanation is rooted in social considerations in the upbringing of males and females.

Men and women differ biologically, and hormonal differences have been explored to assess the origin of the different risk attitudes in the male and female population. Hormonal differences are likely to make men more risk seeking (Brooks et al., 2019) and more overconfident (Fisher & Yao, 2017).

The possibility that societal dynamics might be responsible for the pattern showing females more risk tolerant considers that gender differences are not present at all ages: Booth and Nolen (2012) find that girls in single-sex schools are not differently risk seeking than boys at single- or mixed schools, but girls in mixed school are significantly more risk averse than boys, concluding that social learning might be at play in explaining gender differences in adults.

Marinelli et al. (2017) look at a sample of 2374 clients (1428 males and 946 females) of a large Italian bank to address whether gender differences in risk preferences can be found in real investment decisions and are due to gender alone. Survey data look at different aspects of the investment process and specific attitude (e.g., focusing more on gains or on losses) and are combined with real data on the individuals' portfolios obtained by the banks. The results show that females perceived themselves to be more risk averse than they are but are generally statistically more risk averse than men in the investment decision process even controlling for socio-economic characteristics like age, education, and family dependents. Interestingly, the same differences are captured away by the same controls when looking at portfolio liquidity and diversification.

Montford and Goldsmith (2016) explore whether financial self-efficacy (FSE), defined as "a person's belief about their capability of organizing and executing courses of action to achieve a goal" (ibid, p. 2) can be a factor in explaining the differences in risk preferences between men and women. Using a sample of 182 US undergraduate students, the authors show that once financial self-efficacy is accounted for gender differences tend to disappear: it is the perception regarding one's ability that drives risk tolerance and since women in general tend to have a lower FSE they appear more risk averse.

Regarding **education and financial literacy**, the literature shows that education and risk tolerance tend to be positively correlated. Kannadhasan (2015) shows that more professionally qualified individuals are also more risk tolerant. Being more educated leads household to take on average and above-average financial risk (Huang et al., 2016).

Education may also help to adjust to negative events: Chiang and Xiao (2017) show that being more educated makes individuals less likely to become more risk averse after the 2007 financial crisis.

Bannier and Neubert (2016) show that controlling for financial literacy smooths out differences in risk aversion.

Similarly, financially literate individuals show no significant differences in risk tolerance matter the gender.

Regarding **marital status and economic dependencies**, looking at how couples make joint investment decisions when interacting with an independent financial advisor (Brooks et al., 2019) find that the less risk averse partner (generally the husband) tends to have a stronger impact on the final choice, which is thus closer to the preferences of the more risk tolerant partner. This is true despite the gender of the more risk tolerant partner, although women compromise more than men do; this holds both when they have to accept a riskier allocation and when they manage to induce a riskier allocation. Browne et al. (2016a) explore the implications of changes in family structure on risk tolerance using the German Socio Demographic Panel (SOEP), a representative panel data set surveying roughly 30,000 individuals and 11,000 households since the mid-1980s. Browne and colleagues use four waves of the SOEP (2004, 2006, 2008 and 2012) and use a self-reported measure of risk tolerance. The results show that getting married reduces risk tolerance: individuals who did not marry do not increase their risk aversion as individuals who did. Getting separated increases risk tolerance, but less so for individuals who have children. All these results are significant at statistical level, while getting divorced does not lead to any conclusive results, nor does the death of a life partner. Looking at childbirth, the authors find a marked difference between the birth of the first and following children: having the first child significantly decreases the willingness to take financial risk, while having more children does not produce any statistically significant results. The authors conclude that only the first child produces major changes in future expectations. Individuals who are declared to be the head of the household are less prone to risk-taking and decrease their willingness to take on risk more when having their first child (even excluding single parents). Görlitz and Tamm (2020) find evidence that having a child significantly impacts risk preferences around birth. Looking at the large panel of German households (SOEP) the authors study risk aversion from 4 years before the birth up to 20 years after (waves 2004, 2006 and from 2008 to 2017) using a self-reported measure[11] of risk aversion and several individual controls. In the sample women are more risk averse than men and parents are more risk averse than non-parents. Considering the birth of the first child, results show that women's willingness to take risks starts decreasing already one year before the pregnancy, with the effect slowly fading away at the end of the fourth year after the pregnancy. For men the anticipatory effect on risk preferences starts two years before the pregnancy, reducing the willingness to take risk for up to nine years, although to a much lower level than in the case of women. The paper finds no similar effects for a second child. Controlling for household income, marital status, home ownership, and labor market participation does not change the results. Controlling for age slightly changes the results, in that both genders now feature a decrease in willingness to take risk up to 7–9 years after the first birth.

Health is positively correlated with risk tolerance; in fact, countries where full national health coverage is provided are characterized by a higher general level of risk tolerance (Atella, 2012). Life expectancy and health are both significantly and positively correlated to risk tolerance (Hammitt et al., 2009). A poor general or mental health reduces the disposition to invest in stocks (Jones et al., 2018). Using a large sample of American household in 2004, Hammitt et al. (2009) explore the relationship between health, longevity, and financial risk tolerance. The survey uses a self-reported measure of health and two hypothetical questions drawn from the Health and Retirement study. These questions propose to choose between different jobs that provide different income

[11] They use the same question used in Browne et al. (2016a, 2016b): "How do you see yourself: Are you generally a person who is willing to take risks or do you try to avoid risks? Please answer on a scale from 0 to 10, where 0 means 'not at all willing to take risks' and 10 means 'very willing to take risks'".

streams[12] and allow to classify participants into three risk tolerance categories. The survey results show that both life expectancy and good health are positively and significantly correlated to risk tolerance.

4.2 *Life Events*

Bucciol and Zarri (2015) use data from 4 waves of the US Health and Retirement study and look at the impact of negative events; they show that while both physical attacks and the loss of a child have a significant and negative impact on financial risk tolerance, only the latter has a long-lasting effect.

Chiang and Xiao (2017) focus on the effect of the 2007–2009 financial crisis in the United States on participants in the Survey of Consumer Finances. Risk tolerance is measured objectively, focusing on the share of stocks present in privately managed accounts. The study also uses a subjective measure of willingness to take risks, defined through the selection of one of the following levels of risks: no financial risk, average risk, above-the-average risk, and substantial risk. Among the household characteristics that shift objective risk tolerance downward in 2009 compared to 2007 (pre financial crisis) the authors identify being a minority (Black or Latino) and having a poor health, while higher education levels, higher wealth, and being older than 60 make the downwards shift less likely. Being wealthy and over 60 years old makes it less likely that risk tolerance is shifted upward, which suggests that these categories tend to have more stable preferences that are not influenced by external economic conditions. This result is the only one that is preserved when considering the subjective measure of risk tolerance, while the significance of most of the other parameters disappears.

Using a panel of Australian individuals (Kettlewell, 2019) explores the effects of several life events by looking at 4810 individuals participating

[12] The first question asks "Suppose that you are the only income earner in the family and that you have a good job guaranteed to give you your current income every year for life. You are given the opportunity to take a new and equally good job for life with a 50–50 chance that it will either double your income or cut it by a third. Would you take the new job?". If the first gamble is accepted the respondent is asked "Suppose the chances were 50–50 that it would either double your income or cut it by half. Would you take the new job?"; if the first gamble is not accepted the respondent is asked "Suppose the chances were 50–50 that it would either double your income or cut it by a fifth. Would you take the new job?".

in 8 waves taking part in the survey (years included are 2006, 2008 and from 2010 to 2016) and using a self-reported measure of financial risk tolerance[13] taken from the US Survey of Consumer Finance. The life events considered are major improvement in finances, major worsening in finances, serious personal injury or illness, birth of first child, victim of property crime, death of spouse or child. The survey asks whether each event has occurred in the previous 12 months and, if so, further asks precisely when. Results show that life events impact significantly risk preferences, but that their effect fades over time. Experiencing a major improvement in finance in the last 3–6 months leads to being 1.6 times more likely in a higher risk preference category, but the effect fades in less than 3 years. A financial loss increases risk aversion, and the effect lingers beyond the 3-year interval. Adverse health shocks seem to have a minor impact on risk preferences that fade within a year. Having a first child increases risk aversion, the more so the closer the birth is. In general, the authors find that life events affect risk preferences temporarily and that these effects are felt more strongly by individuals that are less emotionally stable.

4.3 *Behavioral and Personality Factors*

Wong and Carducci (2016) find that *sensation seeking* is positively correlated with risk tolerance. Moreover, the relationship is so strong that it is not mitigated by the effects of gender, age, GPA achievements, and

[13] The question used is the following. Which of the following statements comes closest to describing the amount of financial risk that you are willing to take with your spare cash? That is, cash used for savings or investment.

Participants can choose from the following responses (emphasis not added).

1. I take substantial financial risks expecting to earn substantial returns.
2. I take above-average financial risks expecting to earn above-average returns.
3. I take average financial risks expecting to earn average returns.
4. I am not willing to take any financial risks.
5. I never have any spare cash.

In the waves used in this study, people who choose option 5 are given the following follow-up question.

Assume you had some spare cash that could be used for savings or investment. Which of the following statements comes closest to describing the amount of financial risk that you would be willing to take with this money?

They are then asked to choose from 1 to 4 above.

academic standings in college. The authors also find a positive relationship between *locus of control*[14] and risk tolerance, but this time the relationship holds only for males, older and upper-class individuals (Kesavayuth et al., 2018) find locus of control is positively correlated with higher willingness to take risk for older females but not for males. Kesavayuth et al. (2018) explore the role of a non-cognitive factor on the risk preferences of Australian individuals participating in Household, Income and Labour Dynamics (HILDA) survey.[15] The results show that the locus of control index positively correlates with self-reported willingness to take risks only for some subgroups of the population, namely older females, but has a minor and often non-significant impact on other groups.

Males tend to be more *overconfident* than females and there is a positive relationship between risk seeking/tolerance and overconfidence (Fisher & Yao, 2017).

Bucciol and Zarri (2017) explore the role of personality traits in risk-taking behavior using different waves of the Health and Retirement Survey and find that Agreeableness is negatively correlated with the decision to hold stocks. De Bortoli et al. (2019) find that openness to new experiences is positively related to risk aversion, confirming previous results mentioned in an earlier section.

4.4 Risk Tolerance: Stable Trait or Adaptive Feature?

Gerrans et al. (2015) focus on the period around the global financial crisis (2007–2009) and use data from a large sample of investors from the United States, Australia, and the United Kingdom and show that even though there is general decrease in risk tolerance scores, the mean individual change is very small and not statistically significant, suggesting risk tolerance is more akin to a stable trait.

Schildberg-Hörisch (2018) provides a very important theoretical contribution for the stability of risk preferences. Even if individual risk preferences appear to be persistent and moderately stable over time, their degree of stability is too low to be reconciled with the assumption of perfect stability in neoclassical economic theory. Research in personality

[14] Being low in locus of control implies believing that external factors are mostly responsible for the outcomes we face.

[15] HILDA is an annual survey of a representative sample of Australians. Subsequent waves contribute to constituting a large longitudinal dataset.

psychology provides a framework for preference stability that accommodates evidence on systematic changes in risk preferences over the life cycle, due to exogenous shocks, to temporary changes in self-control resources, emotions, or stress. As far as theory is concerned, research on the stability of risk preferences might ultimately result in an overarching model of endogenous risk preferences in which risk preferences evolve over time as a function of, among others, aging, exogenous shocks, and changes in the decision environment that encompasses situational factors such as the current level of self-control, stress, or emotions.

Another relevant contribution in this regard is the paper by Frey et al. (2017). The authors develop a comprehensive psychometric framework that comprises 39 measures that represent a broad sample of popular measures in research on risk preference. This comprehensive questionnaire is submitted to 1507 healthy adults aged 20–36 years. The results suggest that risk preference has a psychometric structure akin to other major psychological traits, such as intelligence. It involves both a general, stable component that can account for about half of the explained variance and a series of facets, each capturing more specific aspects of risk preference. These results contribute to the debate about the domain-specific nature of risk preference and indicate that this construct encompasses both general and domain-specific components.

Box 1 The practitioner's view: In this box, Giuseppe Amitrano (WieldMore Investment Management) discusses how the novelties introduced by MiFID and MiFID2 changed the financial professionals' operativity and describes the major challenges they had to face

Was the development of a suitability questionnaire an easy process? Which type of guidance was provided? By whom? Did the introduction of the questionnaire change the approach with clients in general, if so, how?

From the financial advisor's perspective, the suitability questionnaire relies on two pillars: the requirements of the Regulations and the risk assessment experience of the financial advisor that can be supported by compliance specialists and technology companies providing methodologies and templates to be incorporated in the questionnaire

The assessment of the questionnaire and its outcome define the level of risk and thus the matching type of instruments that the advisor will suggest to the client. It supports the discussion with the client and provides a clear structure the client is comfortable with. Its introduction was very important as it helped maintain the highest level of customer protection and service

The questionnaire systematizes information about the client but it "does not tell the whole story," as the client's knowledge strongly relies on the personal investor-advisor relation. However, the novelty introduced by the suitability questionnaire is that some details that were considered private in the past by customers are now shared as condition *sine qua non* to open an account

Did compliance become a burden?

In my personal experience, the benefits of using the questionnaire outweighed the efforts needed to be invested into it and thus compliance was not perceived as a burden

Indeed, compliance implies high costs, and in this sense, it can represent a burden. As an example, HSBC employs 11% of workforce in compliance and the role of compliance officers has become more and more important over time. Since rules, laws, and guidelines have multiplied, there's a strong need to have someone supervising organizations from the inside. One of the key challenges in the years to come will be to simplify procedures using technology, and that would ease companies' duties

Was the transition to MiFID2 smooth? How and why? What were the key issues?

The transition leading to the introduction of the first round of MiFID regulations was long and painful, affecting the relationships between different European countries participating in the consultation process, multiplying the number of committees, and governmental institutions involved in the negotiations, led by the European Council and the European Parliament

The prevailing points of discussions in the process were the financial instruments traded in the relative markets affected by MiFID, the scope of products covered and most importantly the relationship among all different stakeholders participating in the negotiations. How to distribute the power between Brussels and the various single member states, their capabilities to preserve their discretionary power, and their independence represented recurrent elements of discussion and decision-making

An important objective of MiFID was to create a framework for transparency where investors could gather all market information getting access to the whole market of products and services and not only what was on offer at the local stock exchange, allowing investors to get the best prices in the market. This generated a tremendous impact on the geography of the investment markets. In few European countries such as France, Italy, and Spain, existing rules concentrated share trading forcing it through local stock exchanges. Instead, the London Stock Exchange in the United Kingdom earned high sums from selling market information. The new MiFID rules put finally the word end to those monopolies

However, the data transparency promised by the initial spirit of the MiFID regulation took too long to materialize: many large financial institutions dragged their feet, because of the time, resources, and costs necessary to implement the new regulatory framework. The regulator appeared too lenient with the large trading facilities, increasing the cost of accessing and transparency of data promised

The transition to MiFID2 meant even higher costs and charges for firms, regarding several aspects of financial services, including reporting, governance, and research. Nevertheless, this helped regulators access better information and intervene more effectively in more recent cases. Investment management companies and product distributors worked hard to ensure they would have been able to meet the obligations outlined by MiFID2 but this again required time, especially for smaller firms. One of the key aspects was that the regulator found a way, through the implementation of the MiFID regulation to delegate the responsibility to the distributors for the product governance rules and for providing information to product manufacturers to ensure that the products were distributed correctly

How did the new compliance rules (including the recognition of independent advisory) affect your field?

The United Kingdom anticipated MiFID2 provision of advice provided on an independent basis with the Retail Distribution Review in the United Kingdom (2012), where it asked firms to define their advice service either as "independent" or "restricted"

The idea to avoid conflicts of interest and work in an open-architecture scheme required stronger compliance policies to ensure clients' protection. The increasing focus on consumer protection made it mandatory to disclose and present ex-ante and ex-post costs and charges which resulted in compressed margins. Nevertheless, there are still many areas to be defined to ensure a greater service and the highest consumer protection. In 2018 BEUC (The European Consumer Organization) carried out a study throughout several countries in Europe ("The Price of Bad Advice") and it pointed out that regulation in Europe is not able to cover investors' needs and is sometimes obsolete in the rapidly changing financial services

How did the new rules change, if ever, your view of clients' needs and how you interact with them?
MiFID2 has not changed the world and in the end business has continued as usual, albeit with materially higher overheads

However, a big step forward in terms of accommodating clients' needs through rule changes can only happen when the attention is shifted from the investment products to the clients' capabilities. It is fundamental to link the general knowledge, experience, and financial education of the investors, with the product, providing products that are understood and fair to the clients

It is thanks to these rules that we as professionals can move from protection to enhancement of the investors and to the definition of rules of conduct and engagement with the market players

5 Taking Stock and Looking at the Challenges Ahead

This chapter explored in detail the interconnections between the regulatory requirements regarding the measurement of financial risk tolerance and the empirical literature. We showed how the suitability questionnaire evolved from a general list of prescriptions in MiFID to a more well-defined list of empirically relevant items in MiFID2, although we highlighted significant variability in the way in which new concepts (especially knowledge about financial topics and ability to bear losses) are being implemented. The last section reviewing further empirical insights from academic papers suggests that risk tolerance continues to be an ever-evolving concept, but that it is now transitioned to a multi-layered one where interconnections among determinants and non-monetary considerations are set to play an even larger role. A case in point is the fact that ESMA mentions considering the outcome of studies in behavioral finance as one of the criteria used when introducing the revised guidelines on suitability in 2018. The next step in this process of convergence between theory and practice is being outlined once again by ESMA, which released new and improved guidelines in January 2022 to further refine the efficacy and effectiveness of suitability questionnaire (European Securities and Markets Authority, 2022). In particular, the new guidelines address a key process that has been taking place in European financial markets—the transition to sustainable financial markets. While this transition is a challenge on its own, it also poses important questions to financial market participants: how is sustainability going to interact with suitability and the assessment of financial risk tolerance? The next chapter will take on this very important question.

References

Anderson, L. R., & Mellor, J. M. (2009). Are risk preferences stable? comparing an experimental measure with a validated survey-based measure. *Journal of Risk and Uncertainty, 39*(2), 137–160. https://doi.org/10.1007/s11166-009-9075-z

Banks, J., Bassoli, E., and Mammi, I. (2020). Changing attitudes to risk at older ages: The role of health and other life events. *Journal of Economic Psychology, 79*(December 2018), 102208. https://doi.org/10.1016/j.joep.2019.102208

Bannier, C. E., & Neubert, M. (2016). Gender differences in financial risk taking: The role of financial literacy and risk tolerance. *Economics Letters, 145*, 130–135. https://doi.org/10.1016/j.econlet.2016.05.033

Bateman, H., Islam, T., Louviere, J., Satchell, S., & Thorp, S. (2011). Retirement investor risk tolerance in tranquil and crisis periods: Experimental survey evidence. *Journal of Behavioral Finance, 12*(4), 201–218. https://doi.org/10.1080/15427560.2011.620199

Bateman, H., Thorp, S., Louviere, J. J. J., Islam, T., & Satchell, S. E. (2012). An Experimental Survey of Investment Decisions for Retirement Savings. *SSRN Electronic Journal*. https://doi.org/10.2139/ssrn.1665943

Bertocchi, G., Brunetti, M., & Torricelli, C. (2011). Marriage and other risky assets: A portfolio approach. *Journal of Banking and Finance, 35*(11), 2902–2915. https://doi.org/10.1016/j.jbankfin.2011.03.019

Blanchett, D., Finke, M., & Guillemette, M. (2018). The Effect of Advanced Age and Equity Values on Risk Preferences. *Journal of Behavioral Finance, 19*(4), 434–441. https://doi.org/10.1080/15427560.2018.1431884

Bogan, V. L., & Fertig, A. R. (2013). Portfolio choice and mental health. *Review of Finance, 17*(3), 955–992. https://doi.org/10.1093/rof/rfs016

Bonsang, E., & Dohmen, T. (2015). Risk attitude and cognitive aging. *Journal of Economic Behavior and Organization, 112*, 112–126. https://doi.org/10.1016/j.jebo.2015.01.004

Booth, A. L., & Nolen, P. (2012). Gender differences in risk behaviour: Does nurture matter? *Economic Journal, 122*(558), 56–78. https://doi.org/10.1111/j.1468-0297.2011.02480.x

Breuer, W., Riesener, M., and Salzmann, A. J. (2014). Risk aversion vs. individualism: what drives risk taking in household finance? *European Journal of Finance, 20*(5), 446–462. https://doi.org/10.1080/1351847X.2012.714792

Brooks, C., Sangiorgi, I., Hillenbrand, C., & Money, K. (2019). Experience wears the trousers: Exploring gender and attitude to financial risk. *Journal of Economic Behavior and Organization, 163*, 483–515. https://doi.org/10.1016/j.jebo.2019.04.026

Browne, M. J., Jaeger, V., Richter, A., & Steinorth, P. (2016a). *Familiy transitions and risk attitude*. Munich Risk and Insurance Center.

Browne, M. J., Jaeger, V., Richter, A., & Steinorth, P. (2016b). Familiy transitions and risk attitude. *SSRN Electronic Journal*. https://doi.org/10.2139/ssrn.2710688

Brunnermeier, M. K., & Nagel, S. (2008). Do wealth fluctuations generate time-varying risk aversion? Micro-evidence on individuals' asset allocation. *American Economic Review, 98*(3), 713–736. https://doi.org/10.1257/aer.98.3.713

Bucciol, A., & Zarri, L. (2015). The shadow of the past: Financial risk taking and negative life events. *Journal of Economic Psychology, 48*, 1–16. https://doi.org/10.1016/j.joep.2015.02.006

Bucciol, A., & Zarri, L. (2017). Do personality traits influence investors' portfolios? *Journal of Behavioral and Experimental Economics, 68*, 1–12. https://doi.org/10.1016/j.socec.2017.03.001

Cameron, L. (2010). Risk taking behavior in the wake of natural disasters. *Journal of Human Resources, 50*(2), 485–515.

Chiang, T. F., & Xiao, J. J. (2017). Household characteristics and the change of financial risk tolerance during the financial crisis in the United States. *International Journal of Consumer Studies, 41*(5), 484–493. https://doi.org/10.1111/ijcs.12356

Commission of the European Communities. (2006). Commmission Directive 2006/73/EC of 10 August 2006. *Official Journal of the European Union, 49*(L241), 26–58.

De Bortoli, D., Da Costa, N., Goulart, M., & Campara, J. (2019). Personality traits and investor profile analysis: A behavioral finance study. *PLoS ONE, 14*(3), 1–18. https://doi.org/10.1371/journal.pone.0214062

De Palma, A., and Picard, N. (2010). *Evaluation of MiFID questionnaires in France Study for the Autorité des Marchés Financiers*.

Dohmen, T., Falk, A., Golsteyn, B. H. H., Huffman, D., & Sunde, U. (2017). Risk Attitudes Across The Life Course. *Economic Journal, 127*(605), F95–F116. https://doi.org/10.1111/ecoj.12322

Dohmen, T., Falk, A., Huffman, D., Sunde, U., Schupp, J., & Wagner, G. G. (2011). Individual risk attitudes: Measurement, determinants, and behavioral consequences. *Journal of the European Economic Association, 9*(3), 522–550. https://doi.org/10.1111/j.1542-4774.2011.01015.x

ESMA. (2012). Guidelines on certain aspects of the MiFID suitability requirements. *European Securities and Markets Authority*, August. https://www.esma.europa.eu/sites/default/files/library/esma35-43-1163_guidelines_on_certain_aspects_of_mifid_ii_suitability_requirements_0.pdf

ESMA. (2018). *Final Report Guidelines on certain aspects of the MiFID II suitability requirements.*

European Parliament and Council of the European Union. (2014a). Directive 2014/65/EU on markets in financial instruments and amending Directive 2002/92/EC and Directive 2011/61/EU. In *Official Journal of the European Union* (Vol. 57, Issue L173, pp. 349–496).

European Parliament and Council of the European Union. (2014b). *Regulation 600/2014 on markets in financial instruments* (Vol. 2014, Issue 600).

European Securities and Markets Authority. (2022). *Consultation Paper Guidelines on certain aspects of the MiFID II suitability requirements. January*. www.esma.europa.eu

Falk, A., Becker, A., Dohmen, T., Enke, B., Huffman, D., and Sunde, U. (2018). Global evidence on economic preferences. *Quarterly Journal of Economics, 133*(4). https://doi.org/10.1093/qje/qjs020.Advance

Fisher, P. J., & Yao, R. (2017). Gender differences in financial risk tolerance. *Journal of Economic Psychology, 61*, 191–202. https://doi.org/10.1016/j.joep.2017.03.006

Frey, R., Pedroni, A., Mata, R., Rieskamp, J., & Hertwig, R. (2017). Risk preference shares the psychometric structure of major psychological traits. *Science Advances, 3*(10), 1–14. https://doi.org/10.1126/sciadv.1701381

Gerrans, P., Faff, R., & Hartnett, N. (2015). Individual financial risk tolerance and the global financial crisis. *Accounting and Finance, 55*(1), 165–185. https://doi.org/10.1111/acfi.12053

Görlitz, K., and Tamm, M. (2020). Parenthood, risk attitudes and risky behavior. *Journal of Economic Psychology, 79*(November 2018), 102189. https://doi.org/10.1016/j.joep.2019.102189

Grable, J. E., and Roszkowski, M. J. (2007). Self-assessments of risk tolerance by women and men. *Psychological Reports, 100*(3 I), 795–802. https://doi.org/10.2466/PR0.100.3.795-802

Grable, J., Lytton, R. H., O'Neill, B., Joo, S.-H., & Klock, D. (2006). Risk Tolerance, Projection Bias, Vividness, and Equity Prices. *The Journal of Investing, 15*(2), 68–74. https://doi.org/10.3905/joi.2006.635632

Grable, J. E., & Roszkowski, M. J. (2008). The influence of mood on the willingness to take financial risks. *Journal of Risk Research, 11*(7), 905–923. https://doi.org/10.1080/13669870802090390

Hammitt, J. K., Haninger, K., & Treich, N. (2009). Effects of health and longevity on financial risk tolerance. *GENEVA Risk and Insurance Review, 34*(2), 117–139. https://doi.org/10.1057/grir.2009.6

Huang, T., Xu, X., & Chiang, T. F. (2016). Household expectations for future economy and risk-taking attitudes. *Journal of Financial Counseling and Planning, 27*(1), 109–121. https://doi.org/10.1891/1052-3073.27.1.109

Hübner, G., and Plunus, S. (2013). Accomodating profile dynamism in MifID II. *Revue Bancaire et Financière.*

Huettinger, M., & Krašauskaitė, A. (2020). Will MiFID II tame the investment services industry of the Baltic Tigers? *Qualitative Research in Financial Markets, 12*(3), 315–331. https://doi.org/10.1108/QRFM-12-2018-0141

Kannadhasan, M. (2015). Retail investors' financial risk tolerance and their risk-taking behaviour: The role of demographics as differentiating and classifying factors. *IIMB Management Review, 27*(3), 175–184. https://doi.org/10.1016/j.iimb.2015.06.004

Kesavayuth, D., Ko, K. M., and Zikos, V. (2018). Locus of control and financial risk attitudes. *Economic Modelling*, *72*(July 2017), 122–131. https://doi.org/10.1016/j.econmod.2018.01.010

Kettlewell, N. (2019). Risk preference dynamics around life events. *Journal of Economic Behavior and Organization, 162*, 66–84. https://doi.org/10.1016/j.jebo.2019.04.018

Linciano, N., and Soccorso, P. (2012). *Assessing investors ' risk tolerance* (Discussion Paper), July.

Lippi, A., & Rossi, S. (2020). Run for the hills: Italian investors' risk appetite before and during the financial crisis. *International Journal of Bank Marketing, 38*(5), 1195–1213. https://doi.org/10.1108/IJBM-02-2020-0058

Loonen, T. (2020). Dutch investment advisors' perceptions towards the MiFID II directive. *Journal of Financial Regulation and Compliance, 29*(2), 202–217. https://doi.org/10.1108/JFRC-03-2020-0023

Loonen, T., & Janssen, R. (2022). Implementation of MiFID II investor protection provisions by private banks within the European Union. *Journal of Financial Regulation and Compliance.* https://doi.org/10.1108/JFRC-10-2021-0087

Lyons, A., Neelakantan, U., and Scherpf, E. (2008). Gender and marital differences in wealth and investment decisions. *Journal of Personal Finance*, *6*(4), 57–76.

Marinelli, N., and Mazzoli, C. (2011). *Profiling investors with the MiFID: current practice and future prospects.* In Mazzoli, Camilla and Marinelli, Nicoletta, an insight into the suitability practice: The Standard Questionnaire Dilemma, January 10, 2011.

Marinelli, N., Mazzoli, C., & Palmucci, F. (2017). How does gender really affect investment behavior? *Economics Letters, 151*, 58–61. https://doi.org/10.1016/j.econlet.2016.12.006

Mata, R., Josef, A. K., & Hertwig, R. (2016). Propensity for risk taking across the life span and around the globe. *Psychological Science, 27*(2), 231–243. https://doi.org/10.1177/0956797615617811

Mayfield, C., Perdue, G., & Wooten, K. (2008). Investment management and personality type. *Financial Services Review, 17*, 219–236.

Mazzoli, C., and Marinelli, N. (2014). Determinants of risk-suitable investment portfolios: Evidence from a sample of Italian householders. *Journal of Economic and Financial Studies, 2*(01), 50. https://doi.org/10.18533/jefs.v2i01.128

Montford, W., & Goldsmith, R. E. (2016). How gender and financial self-efficacy influence investment risk taking. *International Journal of Consumer Studies, 40*(1), 101–106. https://doi.org/10.1111/ijcs.12219

Neelakantan, U. (2010). Estimation and impact of gender differences in risk tolerance. *Economic Inquiry, 48*(1), 228–233. https://doi.org/10.1111/j.1465-7295.2009.00251.x

Outreville, J. F. (2015). The relationship between relative risk aversion and the level of education: A survey and implications for the demand for life insurance. *Journal of Economic Surveys, 29*(1), 97–111. https://doi.org/10.1111/joes.12050

Page, L., Savage, D. A., & Torgler, B. (2014). Variation in risk seeking behaviour following large losses: A natural experiment. *European Economic Review, 71*, 121–131. https://doi.org/10.1016/j.euroecorev.2014.04.009

Roszkowski, M., & Davey, G. (2010). Risk perception and risk tolerance changes attributable to the 2008 economic crisis: A subtle but critical difference. *Journal of Financial Service Professionals, 64*(4), 42–53.

Sahm, C. R. (2012). How much does risk tolerance change? *Quarterly Journal of Finance, 2*(4). https://doi.org/10.1142/S2010139212500206

Schildberg-Hörisch, H. (2018). Are risk preferences stable? *Journal of Economic Perspectives, 32*(2), 135–154. https://doi.org/10.1257/jep.32.2.135

Schurer, S. (2015). Lifecycle patterns in the socioeconomic gradient of risk preferences. *Journal of Economic Behavior and Organization, 119*, 482–495. https://doi.org/10.1016/j.jebo.2015.09.024

Valiante, D., and Assi, B. (2011). MiFID Implementation in the midst of the Financial Crisis Results of an ECMI Survey. In *Regulation*.

Van de Venter, G., Michayluk, D., & Davey, G. (2012). A longitudinal study of financial risk tolerance. *Journal of Economic Psychology, 33*(4), 794–800. https://doi.org/10.1016/j.joep.2012.03.001

van Rooij, M., Lusardi, A., & Alessie, R. (2011). Financial literacy and stock market participation. *Journal of Financial Economics, 101*(2), 449–472. https://doi.org/10.1016/j.jfineco.2011.03.006

Wong, A., & Carducci, B. (2016). Do sensation seeking, control orientation, ambiguity, and dishonesty traits affect financial risk tolerance? *Managerial Finance, 42*(1), 34–41. https://doi.org/10.1108/MF-09-2015-0256

Yao, R., & Hanna, S. D. (2005). The effect of gender and marital status on financial risk tolerance. *Journal of Personal Finance, 4*(1), 66–85.

CHAPTER 3

Challenges and Opportunities in the Regulation of Financial Instruments Post-MiFID2—Sustainable Finance

Abstract This chapter discusses one of the key trends that have swept across the financial world since the introduction of MiFID2—the shift toward sustainable finance—to discuss its relevance for the possible revision of investor protection and suitability rules especially for what concerns the measurement of risk tolerance in current and potential investors. This chapter starts by taking stock of the key regulatory modifications that are creating a convergence between the MiFID world and the sustainability domain, presenting the relevant legislation, and discussing its implications for financial decision-making and risk tolerance.

Keywords Sustainability preferences · ESG · Investor protection

1 Sustainable Finance in a Sustainable Union

1.1 Sustainable Development in the European Union Legislation

Chapter 2 reviewed the key steps in the regulatory definition of suitability—the main dimension in which a potential investor's knowledge and experience, financial situation, including the ability to bear losses and investment horizon including risk tolerance. While a partial convergence between empirical academic studies and content of the regulation can be

© The Author(s), under exclusive license to Springer Nature Switzerland AG 2022

C. Cruciani et al., *Understanding Financial Risk Tolerance*,
https://doi.org/10.1007/978-3-031-13131-8_3

noted, several issues still exist in the actual implementation of the suitability requirements by market participants. This chapter considers that the evolution of the concept of suitability does not occur in a vacuum but is likely to come across several other pieces of legislation that might affect the way in which investors approach and deal with investment opportunities. In January 2022 the European Securities and Markets Authority (ESMA) released a new revised version of the guidelines for the implementation of the suitability requirements where it explicitly addresses how MiFID2 is going to interact with the new legislative changes in terms of the transition of the European Union to a zero-carbon future (European Securities & Markets Authority, 2022).

The transition to a more sustainable finance has been at the core of the EU strategy regarding sustainable development since the signing of the Kyoto Protocol in 2008. The European Union has introduced sustainable development as one of its core objectives in the Treaty on the European Union and has been a vocal and active player in international negotiations supporting the Sustainable Development Goals and the recent signing of the Paris Accord. This political will has translated also into a significant legislative effort, whose broad scope and intended coverage intersect with current legislation on European financial markets. The following section will highlight the formal effort of the European Union in realizing its sustainable future, suggesting which are the contact points with MiFID2 and its principles.

1.2 From Theory to Action: The EU Action Plan on Sustainable Development

At the end of 2016, the European Commission took a step forward in shaping the features of the new sustainable financial framework by appointing a High-level Expert Group on sustainable finance tasked with identifying the key steps to build a European sustainable-finance framework.

These key recommendations became the backbone of the **Action Plan on Sustainable Finance** that was released in March 2018 (European Commission, 2018). The Action Plan defines sustainable finance as the "process of taking due account of environmental and social considerations in investment decision-making, leading to increased investments in longer-term and sustainable activities" (ibid, p. 3) and is considered to have the potential to impact all segments of the economy, as capital flows are key to support all sorts of economic activities, thereby affecting both the job market and the long-term growth prospects of the Union members. The Action Plan identified three main objectives and defined for each one a set of actions: re-orienting capital flows toward sustainable investment to foster sustainable and inclusive growth (5 related actions); managing sustainability risks, especially for what concerns environmental and social implications (3 related actions); shifting the development paradigm toward a longer-term horizon, as deemed necessary to pursue sustainable growth (2 related actions). Each Action also includes a timeline for its implementation, which, as will be shown in the next sections, was largely respected.

Concerning the first goal to re-orient financing toward sustainable projects, the Action Plan highlighted the lack of agreement on how much investment is needed yearly, with estimates ranging from the €180 billion a year calculated by the EC in 2016 to support the EU's current energy policy to over €270 billions calculated by the European Investment Bank in 2016. Since then, the decision to take up more ambitious climate-related goals has pushed up the financing gap to over €300 billions a year.[1] The Action Plan proposed to attract this massive flow of resources through two key avenues: public and private investment. On one side, the Plan proposes to strengthen the direct involvement of the EU in financing the shift toward a more sustainable finance through public support devoting a share of the EU budget to Climate and Environment expenditures. On the side of private investment, the European Fund for Strategic Investment (EFSI)[2] is set to play a role in attracting further private funding to develop sustainable infrastructures, although the bulk of private investment will be indirectly pursued by further effort in creating a shared language and metrics around sustainable investment. The measures to be implemented to fulfill the transition to a greener economy are many and will be briefly detailed in the following section.

[1] https://www.bruegel.org/2020/01/a-trillion-reasons-to-scrutinise-the-green-deal-investment-plan/, accessed on May 30, 2022.

[2] The EFSI was established in 2015 as part of the Investment Plan for Europe to be later extended until the end of 2020 in 2017 with the goal of mobilizing half a trillion of additional investment. The EFSI has been replaced by the InvestEU program, which will be discussed in Section X.

1.3 Setting the Plan into Action

As previously mentioned, the EU Action Plan on Sustainable Investment laid out timelines for addressing and legislating on each one of the 10 Actions included in the Plan. The operationalization of this broad vision of a sustainable future for European finance has seen significant progress since the publication of the Action Plan in coherence with the EU Green Deal approved only a year after the Action Plan. The rest of this section will highlight the progress in key areas for investor protection and financial advisory, to broaden the discussion of how sustainability may affect risk tolerance and the uptake of financial products and advice. Thus, actions that are only tangentially related to investor protection and financial advice provision will be summarized, while more relevant actions will be discussed more thoroughly.

1.3.1 Goal 1—Re-Orienting Investment Toward Sustainable Finance

Action 1—Establishing an EU Classification System for Sustainable Activities

Adopted in June 2020, the EU Taxonomy for sustainable activities (European Parliament and the Council, 2020) officially entered into force on July 12, 2020. Article 3 of the EU Taxonomy clearly sets out the criteria that allow to identify an environmentally sustainable activity as an activity that contributes substantially and does not harm the pursuit of the environmental objectives[3] set out in the Directive, and is carried out in compliance with minimum safeguards and complies with the technical screening criteria. One of the most significant contributions of this Directive is the definition of technical screening criteria for each environmental objective to come up with a list of environmentally sustainable activities. A series of Delegated acts[4] adopted in 2021 and early 2022

[3] This is the list of environmental objectives as defined in Art. 9 of the EU Taxonomy: (a) climate change mitigation; (b) climate change adaptation; (c) the sustainable use and protection of water and marine resources; (d) the transition to a circular economy; (e) pollution prevention and control; and (f) the protection and restoration of biodiversity and ecosystems.

[4] Delegated acts are adopted by the European Commission after a relatively short period of time since the initial draft is published, allowing for stakeholders to respond to any request for feedback and advice. The European Parliament and Council normally vote

have provided the criteria for the identification of environmentally sustainable economic activities in different sectors, starting from the ones more closely related to the process of achieving climate neutrality and increasing adaptation to climate change. The EU Taxonomy includes some mandatory disclosure requirements carefully defined in a Delegated act, which requires, for instance, that large financial and nonfinancial corporations and financial-markets participants like asset managers to disclose information about how their activities meet the EU Taxonomy criteria (European Commission, 2021a). The EU Taxonomy also establishes the Platform on Sustainable Finance that involves different stakeholders including EU Agencies and bodies such as the European Environmental Agency and experts representing academia or relevant private stakeholders whose main task will be to support the European Commission in the definition and monitoring of the technical screening criteria, especially for what concerns their application. The EU Taxonomy will be formally reviewed in July 2023 and every three years afterward to evaluate its scope and applicability (Art. 26).

Action 2: Creating Standards and Labels for Green Financial Products

The European Commission started working on the development of the EU Ecolabel for retail financial products in 2018. The Eu Ecolabel is a large initiative that encompasses many different categories of products that minimize their environmental impact according to periodically revised criteria. The latest available draft documentation on the European Commission website dates back to March 2021. Konstantas et al. (2021) indicates that to qualify for this Ecolabel, investment funds must invest a large share of their assets[5] in activities that qualify as environmentally sustainable according to the EU Taxonomy directive.

Another activity in compliance with this goal is the development of an EU green-bond standard. The current proposed framework, introduced in July 2021, defines a voluntary framework supervised by ESMA, characterized by transparent and detailed reporting and aligned with the EU Taxonomy (European Commission, 2021c).

after a period of four months to accept the Delegated Acts as they are proposed, no amendments are possible.

[5] The share ranges from 40% for equity funds, 50% for mixed and bond funds, and 70% for alternative investment funds.

Action 3: Fostering Investment in Sustainable Projects
Released at the end of 2019, the European Green Deal is part of a broad strategy to scale up the EU commitment to halting climate change and fostering a transition to a greener and just society (European Commission, 2019b). It is an overarching plan encompassing several different dimensions from cleaner energy production to fostering a circular economy, to improving food systems and encouraging smart mobility. In the December 2019 Communication about the deal, this major shift toward a greener society is estimated to require at least €260 billion per year in additional investment—roughly 1.8% of the 2018 EU GDP (ibid, p. 15). While the original communication set the goal of reducing greenhouse gas emission by 50–55% from 1990 by the year 2030 in order to achieve climate neutrality by 2050, later communications set it firmly at 55%, although the planned policies included in the Communication did come somewhat short of this objective (Fleming & Mauger, 2021). In a Communication released in September 2020, the European Commission committed to dedicating "at least 30% of its firepower to climate-relevant spending" (European Commission, 2020a, 2020b, p. 5) making the financial dimension a key lever for this green transition. It is noteworthy that the goal to pursue this green transition is coupled with the digital transformation needed by European companies and that both are at the core of the Next Generation EU program—the most recent Unionwide program to support companies and spur private investment after the Covid-19 pandemic years. The Communication is explicit in suggesting that public spending is considered a lever to trigger significant private investment.

The mobilization of financial resources to support the EU Green Deal is implemented through the European Green Deal Investment Plan (EGDIP), an ambitious plan to drive around €1 trillion into sustainable investment in the European Union over 10 years starting in 2021.[6] The Plan is structured to be financed primarily through the EU budget, diverting €503 billion from the Climate and Environment budget and €25 billion from the EU Emission Trading System. The rest of the funding would be generated by the interaction between public and private interests in the project financed or guaranteed by the InvestEU program overseen by the European Investment Bank group. Another important

[6] The Plan currently covers the 2021–2027 time frame but assumes that the climate targets post 2027 will be at least maintained.

piece of the financial project is the Just Transition Mechanism (JTM) and, as the name suggests, recognizes that such a bold and transformative shift toward a greener economy may have diverging implications for different Member States. The JTM's activities are mainly targeted to vulnerable workers, SMEs, and jobless individuals, but over time and in response to the Covid-19 crisis its budget[7] has been revised and its scope broadened (Fleming & Mauger, 2021). The JTM is not just about money, but also about technical advice and support: with this in mind the Just Transition Platform, aimed at exchanging information and best practices, was launched in June 2020.

Action 4: Incorporating Sustainability When Providing Financial Advice

The need to develop sound and shared guidelines to spur sustainable finance dates before the introduction of the Action Plan but has found significant momentum in its adoption. In particular, the European Commission tasked a High-Level Expert Group on Sustainable Finance (HLEG) to come up with recommendations to finance a sustainable European economy in December 2016. After a year-long consultation with stakeholders, the HLEG published a final report with its recommendations in January 2018 (EU High-Level Expert Group on Sustainable Finance, 2018) where it explicitly stated that investment advisors should be required "to ask about, and then respond to, retail investors' preferences about the sustainable impact of their investments, as a routine component of financial advice" (ibid, p. 28) calling for a MiFID2 revision to include investors' sustainability preferences into the suitability requirements.[8]

The European Commission published a first Draft to amend the way in which sustainability preferences are accounted for in financial advisory in 2019 (European Commission, 2019a), to which ESMA was called to respond after a public consultation. In its final technical report,

[7] The JTM comprises the Just Transition Fund with current budget equal to €17.5 billion, to which Member States can pledge voluntary contributions, aimed at supporting specific vulnerable areas approved by the EC; the Just Transition Scheme which seeks to attract private investment using a EU budget guarantee; and a public sector loan facility providing concessional loans to public entities relying on the EU budget and mostly on European Investment Bank lending.

[8] The report touches upon many other themes that are not discussed in this section as they pertain to aspects other than financial advice provision.

ESMA (European Securities & Markets Authority, 2019) stresses the importance of well-defined terminology but suggests that sustainability integration should be performed avoiding a too prescriptive approach in order to avoid "the risk of stifling innovation or creating regulatory inconsistencies" (ibid, p. 5).

The final view on the integration of sustainability preferences builds upon the integrated framework regarding sustainable investment that was in place by 2021: alongside the already cited EU Taxonomy, the Regulation on sustainability-related disclosures in the financial services sector (SFDR)[9] had been introduced providing a much more formal structure and common denominators to define sustainable investment activities. The final Delegated Regulation introduced in 2021 (European Commission, 2021b) distinguishes clearly between investment objectives and sustainability preferences stating that "Sustainability factors should not take precedence over a client's personal investment objective" postponing the evaluation of sustainability preferences to after the investment objective has been determined (p. 5). Article 1 includes the mandatory evaluation of a client's sustainability preferences whose outcome should shape the selection process of the investment products. It is important to note that the Delegated Regulation pushes the concept of sustainable development beyond the Eu Taxonomy and the SFDR by providing three categories of sustainable investments allowing investment firms to suggest any relevant (sustainable) investment product that is based on the sustainability concepts included in the Regulations but not limited to sustainable investment funds. Two of the three categories of investment introduced are defined as "a financial instrument for which the client or potential client determines that a minimum proportion shall be invested in sustainable investments (...)[10]" leaving the definition of this minimum level to the client, in order to mirror their sustainability ambitions. Sustainability also becomes relevant for ex-post information disclosure, as it becomes one of the elements the final investment recommendation needs to be aligned with and explained in a written report alongside investment objectives, risk profile, and capacity for experiencing losses. The Delegated Regulation also touches upon the topic of integrating sustainability risk into the risk management of the investment firms. A consultation paper

[9] The SFRD will be discussed more in detail in a later section.

[10] One category refers to the EU Taxonomy and the other to the SFDR.

was released by ESMA in January 2022 (European Securities & Markets Authority, 2022), further clarifying these requirements: in particular, the suggestion provided for the inclusion of sustainability includes collecting information regarding whether the client has sustainability preference; if so, to which sustainability definition they relate and which is the minimum proportion of sustainable investment they desire and whether they wish to consider any principal adverse impact. Information should be clear and effective, non-technical, qualitative assessment of sustainability preferences is also possible. The Delegated Regulation will apply from August 2, 2022.

Action 5: Developing Sustainability Benchmarks
In 2019 the European Commission put forward a revision of the European Benchmark Regulation (Council of the European Union, 2016), which broadly dealt with indices used as benchmarks in financial instruments to measure the performance of investment funds. The rationale for this revision lies in the need to provide more precise definitions regarding the climate-related goal of different benchmarks align to, distinguishing for instance between EU benchmarks and benchmarks aligned to the Paris Agreement goals (European Parliament, 2019). The Regulation clearly calls for "maintaining the proper functioning of the internal market for the benefit of consumers" (ibid, Preamble paragraph 14) and introduces a regulatory framework defining the requirements for using the EU Climate Transition Benchmarks and EU Paris-aligned Benchmarks, which become easy-to-recognize labels to orient investors' choices. Moreover, benchmark administrators are responsible for communicating clearly whether and how the benchmarks pursue ESG objectives and for reviewing the methodologies underlying the benchmarks regularly.

1.3.2 Goal 2—Sustainability in Risk Management

Action 6: Better Integrating Sustainability in Ratings and Market Research
This action is still in progress and is motivated by the consideration that sustainability ratings are going to play a crucial role in fostering the diffusion of sustainable investment, but several key areas still need to be addressed for what concerns the pursuit of the related Action-plan action.

The European Commission tasked Sustainability (a company part of Environmental Resource Management company) to collect and evaluate all the available information on the development of sustainability ratings (ERM, 2020). The study finds that self-regulation is the norm when it comes to sustainability assessment and ratings, as current regulations do not yet provide a comprehensive framework. Providers offer different types of sustainability-assessment tools such as raw data, ratings and rankings, screening services, indices and benchmarks, and climate-specific products using company data coming directly from the covered company, company data from other sources, and in some cases even data from other providers. Lack of available data might push providers to resort to estimates and may require provider-specific data to fine-tune the estimation models. The report highlights that the lack of a standard rating process impacts the burden that sustainable companies face to receive a rating: in particular, it estimates that companies need "316 days per year completing their own company sustainability reports and other disclosures, and an average of 155 days per year responding to and managing sustainability-related ratings and ranking providers" (ibid, p. 9). Common biases in the sustainability-rating estimation procedures analyzed include the size bias, the geographical bias, and the industry bias. As for the former, bigger companies have more resources to dedicate to the data collection for the disclosure than smaller companies, thus accurate and complete reporting is less costly in relative terms. The second bias stems from the fact that some areas of the world are subject to stricter reporting requirements, so they might report more and better information simply because they must. The last bias looks at the fact that industry weights and how individual companies fit within the industry seem oversimplified and might mask important differences that do not show up in ratings. The report concludes with some important recommendations including greater transparency in the procedures, weights, and processes used for the ratings, including how providers address bias and the timing of corrections. Moreover, it would be important to standardize company sustainability reporting beyond the current (largely voluntary) standards to overcome many of the existing differences that increase the complexity of devising sustainability ratings. Finally, the report calls for an improvement in the clarity and precision of the terminology used.

Action 7: Clarifying Institutional Investors' and Asset Managers' Duties

In November 2019, the European Commission adopted a new regulation called the Sustainable Finance Disclosures Regulation (SFDR) regarding sustainability-related disclosures in the financial services sector that became applicable in the Union starting on March 10, 2021 (The European Parliament & the Council, 2019). The Directive laid down specific rules regarding the disclosure of sustainable financial products looking at how sustainability affects both internal processes within financial market participants and financial advisors (entity-level dimension) and the performance of financial products (product-level dimension), formalizing pre-contractual and ongoing disclosures to end investors to improve transparency and reduce the informational asymmetries between clients and financial market participants and financial advisors. Regarding transparency over internal processes dealing with sustainable products (entity-level), Directive 2019/2088 required financial market participants and advisers to report on their website how sustainability risks are integrated (Articles 3 and 4), including how the impact of the integration of sustainability risks is mirrored in the remunerations (Article 5). Even if it is not technically a labeling regime, the SFDR requires to state clearly how the stated sustainability ambitions of a financial product are being or are planned to be achieved. The Directive distinguishes between principal adverse impacts of investment decisions, whose impact on sustainability factors must be discussed on the financial market participants' websites, and adverse impacts, which may not be considered on the websites but whose absence needs to be discussed (the "comply or explain" approach) (Article 4).

Regarding product-level requirements of the SFDR Directive, two different levels of sustainable products are defined according to how sustainability is factored into the product development. Article 8 identifies financial products that promote environmental or social characteristics, called light-green products. Transparency requires to include information on how these characteristics are met or on how a benchmark index selected as reference benchmark pursues those same characteristics. Article 9 identifies products that have sustainable investment as an objective and for which an index has been designated as a reference benchmark; transparency for these products requires that information on how the index aligns with the objective is provided (dark-green products). All information regarding so-defined sustainable products needs to be included in the financial market participants' or advisers' websites in a "clear, succinct and understandable to investors" way (Article 10).

SFDR pursued the goal of improving the quality and quantity of information related to sustainable investment products, while increasing the comparability of sustainable investment opportunities but required further clarifications to become fully operational. On February 2, 2021 the Joint Committee of the three European Supervisory Authorities (EBA, EIOPA, and ESMA[11]) released draft Regulatory Technical Standards (RTS) for the implementation of the SFDR (ESA, 2021). The RTS specify which sustainability factors need to be taken in consideration when examining the principal adverse impacts at entity level that consider Climate and Environment-related adverse impacts and adverse impacts in the field of social and employee matters, respect for human rights, and anti-corruption and anti-bribery matters. A mandatory reporting template for the principal adverse impacts is also included in the Annex of the RTS. The RTS also provide clarifications on several product-level requirements of the SFDR: for what concerns pre-contractual disclosures, the standards devised a set of uniform pre-contractual disclosures for the different products listed in SFDR balancing comprehensibility and comprehensiveness and listed in the Annexes. In addition to the mandatory templates in the Annexes among the items that need to be included we find the type of product and how the environmental or social characteristic or the sustainable investment objective of the product are achieved. Moreover in case the financial product complies with the "do not significantly harm" principle from Article 2(17) of SFDR, further information needs to be provided, including discussing the alignment with the OECD Guidelines for Multinational Enterprises and the UN Guiding Principles on Business and Human Rights, including the principles and rights set out in the eight fundamental conventions identified in the Declaration of the International Labour Organization on Fundamental Principles and Rights at Work and the International Bill of Human Rights. This alignment is needed to reconcile the ideal of "do not harm" disclosure in line with the minimum standards under the EU Taxonomy mentioned in an earlier section of this chapter. Product-level disclosures also include website and periodic disclosures. Regarding the former, the Standards discuss the content and presentation of the information that needs to be

[11] Collectively knowns as European Supervisory Authorities or ESA.

included on the website for both Articles 8 and 9 and for products that comply with the "do not significantly harm" principle, for all of which mandatory templates are defined. Periodic disclosures are also covered in the standards, which present a mandatory list of items to be included in the reporting, including information on the success of the product in attaining its environmental or social characteristic or sustainable investment objective, a historical comparison looking at up to five reference periods and the top 15 investments undertaken in a given reference period.

On June 2, 2022, the three European Supervisory Authorities released a clarification note on the RTS (ESA, 2022) that shed light on some more practical matters regarding for instance which indicators can be used to verify the lack of principal adverse impacts and how to properly compute progress along sustainability objectives. Moreover, a notable clarification regards the fact that "financial products that have sustainable investment as an objective should only make sustainable investments" (ibid, p. 6) but that disclosure on (partially) sustainable products should not look only at the sustainable component but also demonstrate that the non-sustainable component does not prevent the product from reaching its sustainable investment objective. Several other points discussed in the clarifications look at pre-contractual and periodic disclosure suggesting practical tips (use of charts or figures, which accounting figures to look at) to facilitate information transparency and clarity. The final list of Adverse sustainability indicators includes in total 9 environmental indicators, 5 social and employee, respect for human rights, anti-corruption and anti-bribery matters indicators and 4 indicators applicable to investments in sovereigns and supranationals. The new version of the SFDR including the RTS is scheduled to enter into force on January 1, 2023.

Action 8: Incorporating Sustainability into Prudential Requirements

The European Banking Authority (EBA) has received the mandate to define guidelines on how sustainability factors can be effectively considered in EU legislation, in order to promote the convergence of different sustainability rules. The EBA released an Action Plan in December 2019 where the timing of the different actions it is working on is described (EBA, 2019). In particular, the EBA is supposed to devise a monitoring system to assess ESG-related material risks, contribute to the definition of standards and benchmarks, understand the role of ESG in risk management, including the impact of ESG on lending and assess the prudential treatment to apply to exposures associated with such ESG objectives. The timeline for the delivery of this complex mandates set 2025 as a tentative deadline, with different actions progressing at once, but mostly starting with strategy and risk management, to then move on to key metrics and disclosure, stress testing and scenario analysis, and lastly to prudential treatment.

1.3.3 Goal 3—Fostering Transparency and Long-Termism

Action 9: Strengthening Sustainability Disclosure and Accounting Rulemaking

The European Union first introduced nonfinancial reporting with Directive 2014/95 (NonFinancial Reporting Directive or NFRD), amending the Accounting Directive and requiring large public entities with more than 500 employees to disclose information regarding how the company is affected and affects (principle of double materiality) four domains of sustainability: environment, social and employee issues, human rights, and bribery and corruption. In the annual documentation, companies needed to provide information on business model, policies, outcomes, risks and risk management, and key performance indicators (KPIs) relevant to the business. Companies produced nonfinancial information reports for the first time in 2018 based on the fiscal year 2017 according to this Directive. A consultation was launched in 2019 (European Commission, 2020b) and highlighted that several steps still needed to be taken to ensure accountability and transparency of nonfinancial information; in particular, the lack of comparability across information provided by different companies for end-investors and the complexity of the decision regarding what to include for companies led to the proposal to develop and use common standards for reporting that include digitalization of all information. Building on this consultation the European Commission adopted a new Directive (the Corporate Sustainability Reporting Directive or CSRD) in April 2021, as scheduled in the Action Plan. The new Directive considers also that the need to improve corporate reporting of sustainability stems not only from users' needs, but also from the new regulations introduced (SFDR and the EU Taxonomy). To be compliant with these new regulations, financial advisors and asset managers require more detailed information on sustainability from the companies whose financial products they place to investors. The proposed new Directive potentially expands the number of covered companies from 11,600 to 49,000 as it includes all large companies and all companies listed in EU-regulated markets excluding micro-companies. For what concerns the costs of reporting by these companies, the Commission estimates that the use of sustainability reporting standards could lead to annual savings of EUR 24,200–41,700 per company, as reporting costs are likely to increase to meet the unregulated demands of end-investors. Moreover, CSRD formalizes the sustainability information that companies need to report and ensures that sustainability information is in line with mandatory EU sustainability reporting standards: in particular, it requires to disclose information regarding the company's business model and strategy including how they are resilient to sustainability risks, the role of the board and management, the principal adverse impacts linked to the company and its value chain, the role of intangibles, and how reported information have been identified. Moreover, it introduced the need to report different types of information: qualitative and quantitative, forward-looking and retrospective, looking at short, medium, and long-term time horizons according to the company. A final important point is that sustainability information will be published as part of companies' management reports in a digital format that is machine readable.

Action 10: Fostering Sustainable Corporate Governance and Attenuating Short-Termism in Capital

This action is mostly targeted to favoring a shift in the general principles shaping corporate governance and has mostly taken the form of a series of consultations with the European Supervisory Agencies to define what it means for companies to overcome short-termism understanding which market practices are more likely to create pressure to companies to rely on such time frame. This action is currently non-legislative, which implies that the adoption of a technical standard should be avoided in favor of directions and suggestions to align corporate governance practices with sustainability goals and properly dealing with sustainability risks within corporations.

1.4 The Action Plan and Investor Protection: Taking Stock and Moving Forward

The comprehensive plan that emerges from the combination of the 10 actions of the European Action Plan is relevant for end investors despite many of the Actions implemented do not target this category directly. Some Actions contribute to strengthening the definitions of what is means to be sustainable across different financial products, ranging from green bond to Ecolabel products or to sustainability benchmarks. Since the plurality of definition is a key concern, as highlighted in several studies mentioned, this move has evident implications also for financial consumers even if it directly affects the firms that wish to produce and place this product.

The Action Plan is targeted at re-orienting financial flows, but it definitely affects information flows across the actors involved in financial markets—including end investors, as shown in Fig. 1.

Actions 1, 7, and 9 define the new information flows related to sustainability that will be created by the combined implementation of the different measures envisaged. Despite not being directly targeted, end-investors will receive from financial advisors and asset managers information on sustainable financial products that financial and nonfinancial

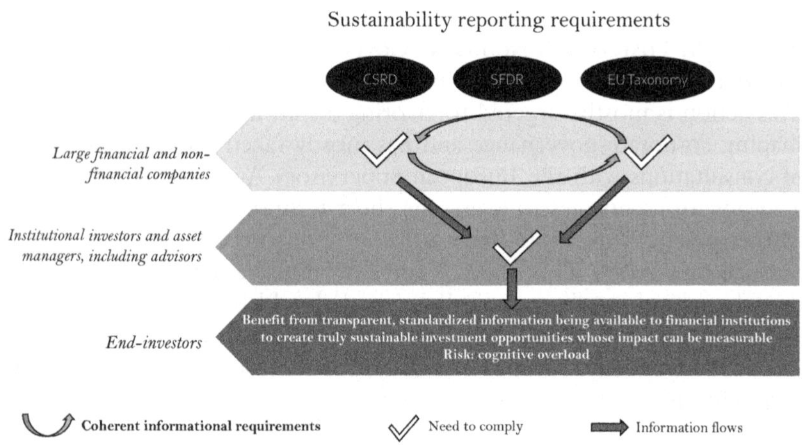

Fig. 1 Information flows and market players affected by sustainability disclosure

companies have developed and about which have completed the mandatory disclosure. Investors are going to access this potentially very rich information flow provided that their sustainability preferences make them suitable for those financial products (Action 4). Thus, it becomes even clearer why sustainability preference assessment is crucial, as it is likely to shape the investment possibility (and the size of the potential information flow) reaching the client. One shortcoming of the increased investor protection and transparency approach in MiFID2 was the risk of causing cognitive overload to clients. An open question regarding sustainability disclosure is whether the objective to reassure clients about the sustainable quality of a product is not counterbalanced by excessive information. The European authorities are clearly motivated by the desire to fight greenwashing, but are (all) clients aware of the problem and worried enough about it to want to navigate this extra stock of information? Talking about greenwashing is also necessary to reflect on whether companies will want to go through the disclosure requirements to reap the extra benefit of being sustainable in a market where not everyone is. The next section takes a look at financial market figures and explores how the described regulation are dealing with greenwashing and driving financial flows toward sustainable companies.

2 Investing in Sustainability—Investor Preferences, Risk Tolerance, and Investment Behavior

2.1 Sustainability Investment—Where Does Europe Stand?

The European Union is not only very active in promoting and regulating sustainable finance, but it is also attracting the largest share of sustainable investment funds in the last few years. According to a recent Morningstar report in the first quarter of 2022 Europe held 82% of all sustainable investment fund investments (Morningstar, 2022a) and looking at data over the last three years confirms that European funds attract the lion's share of sustainable investment. Europe also holds the first place in terms of new sustainable-fund launches (145 new funds accounting for 64% of all launches). Despite these impressive figures, the first quarter of 2022 has seen a significant decrease in sustainable-fund investment in Europe compared to the last quarter of 2021 (where it totaled 124.5 billion) due to increased market volatility linked to the war in Ukraine.

Nevertheless, sustainable funds show more resilience to macroeconomic interferences, displaying lower volatility compared to conventional funds, which recorded a 21 billion net outflow in the same quarter while sustainable funds attracted almost 78 billion in net inflows. Equity continues to represent the largest segment of sustainable funds both in terms of values (60% in Q_4-2021 and 62% in Q_1-2022) and in the number of new funds launched.

A recent assessment of the impact of the SFDR Directive[12] on the supply of investment funds in Europe shows that in the last quarter of 2021 sustainable funds (grouping Articles 9 and 8 together) attracted 64% of all investment funds inflows despite accounting for only 42.4%[13] of the total EU assets in investment funds. There were 200 new Articles 9 and 8 funds, 54% of all new funds launched in Europe in the same quarter. Overall, both Articles 9 and 8 funds are prevalently equity funds. Another interesting change in the supply of sustainable investment products after the introduction of the SFDR is the possibility to reclassify previously Article 6 funds by introducing ESG concerns or sustainability goals and processes in the fund structure. Morningstar found that around 1800 funds were reclassified into either Article 8 or 9 funds. On this respect the report raises some concerns regarding possible greenwashing implications: some newly rebranded Article 8 funds seem to have just received a "light touch" to qualify for the new classification. This implies that no major change in strategy or investment process seems to have been implemented, with many changes amounting to the clarification of already existing ESG implications (Morningstar, 2022b).

The data presented paint a clear picture: investors want sustainable products and the introduction of a framework to clarify what sustainability implies in finance has attracted even more interest. While standards need to be in place to reduce greenwashing risks in theory, in practice the implications of the new regulations will become clear only once another more fundamental question is addressed: what makes investors want to engage in sustainable finance in the first place? Answering this question is

[12] As detailed in a previous section, SFDR distinguishes between Article 6 funds, which do not have a specific sustainability-related goal but still need to disclose some ESG information, Article 8 funds (light green) are supposed to broadly promote environmental and social characteristics, and Article 9 (dark green) have sustainable investment goals and are characterized by investments that do not pose harm to sustainability goals.

[13] This percentage is split between Article 8 funds (37.7%) and Article 9 (4.7%).

the key goal of the next section, which will go back to academic literature and reports to highlight the more prominent dimensions that seem to characterize the sustainable investor.

2.2 *Sustainable Investors—Who Are They and Why Do They Choose Sustainable Products?*

There are several theoretical reasons why investors should hold sustainable investment products ranging from economic to social motives. Among the former, investors may choose sustainable products to further diversify risk in their portfolios, or because they hold extremely high return expectations regarding these products. Social motives span from self-centered ones—the positive effect on reputation or social image—to more other-regarding ones tied to the fact that individuals might be willing to pay a premium to know that their investment is going toward sustainable companies. Puaschunder (2017) presents a comprehensive and thorough literature review of the potentially relevant drivers of sustainable investment within these two categories: the economic motives listed includes rational profit maximization and leadership advantages, while the social ones refer to theories of altruism, innovation, transparency, and social status prospects. A notable aspect of Puaschunder's review is that, especially when it comes to social motives the publications discussed date back at least a decade, suggesting that the concern regarding the socio-psychological motives of sustainable investment has not been a key approach in the study of sustainable investment. Another element to consider is that before the increased effort toward sustainable finance had increased the amount of sustainable investment opportunities, sustainability investment had been seen as a limited form of investment: investors choosing to invest responsibly 15 years ago did not have many options to choose from. Hence the attention of mainstream research was on those investors with unbounded choices, who accounted for most of the investor population.

Understanding why investors choose to invest sustainably has become crucial for two sets of reasons: the first one is the increased and more stringent requirements put in place in what is currently the largest market for sustainable products—the European Union, as was detailed in the previous section. The second reason is that as sustainable investment is set to become mainstream, understanding what sustainable preferences imply is crucial for institutional investors, who make choices for potential individual investors whose preferences they need to anticipate, and for financial advisors, who need to juggle sustainability preferences along with the many other individual features they must keep track of, risk tolerance being the most prominent of all.

This section sets out to review relevant, mostly academic, findings to shed light on the profile of the sustainable investor to provide suggestions and implications for all market players focusing on the two key areas outlines above (economic and social motives) complementing it with demographic information regarding the key features of the sustainable investor.

2.2.1 *Demographic Characteristics*

Several papers include socio-demographic information that contribute to painting the picture of the current sustainable investor. Puaschunder (2017) shows that earlier papers (Hayes, 2001; Rosen et al., 1991; Sparkes, 2002) describe the sustainable investor as well-educated, young, and more likely female and do not find a particular risk profile associated with such investors. Riedl and Smeets (2017) also find that sustainable investors are more likely to hold a university degree and feel more confident about their financial abilities.

Even outside academia, studies confirm that millennials are the generation that is more interested in sustainable investment: 95% of millennials versus 86% of the general population declare interest in such products (Morgan Stanley Institute for Sustainable Investing, 2019), with both being 10% points above the level found in the 2017 version of the study.

2.2.2 *Economic Reasons*

The empirical literature is divided on whether sustainable investment provides better or worse financial results than non-sustainable options. From a theoretical point of view, sustainable funds might face different additional sources of costs compared to conventional funds: a notable one relates to reduced diversification opportunities, especially if the fund uses negative screening as a technique for stock selection.[14]

[14] Negative screening is one of the possible strategies used to compose sustainable investment funds that implies that some sectors (and the relative financial products are excluded). According to Eurosif there are currently 6 responsible investment strategies other than negative screening: best in class, whereby the best ESG performer in a given

It is beyond the scope of this review to discuss all the drivers of risk-adjusted returns of sustainable funds; it suffices to point out that even focusing on this simple and evident dimension—market performance—the literature is still remarkably divided. The discrepancies among the different studies, some of which are mentioned later, can be at least partially explained considering that there are different models to adjust for risk (CAPM, Fama and French 5-factor models, etc.) but remains striking as financial return is notably a very easy to communicate and catchy aspect of a financial product.

Some authors have found that sustainable funds appear to be more resilient in times of crisis: Das et al. (2018) look at the performance of US-based SRI funds from the Morningstar database over the period 2005–2016 and show that funds with higher ESG rating outperformed sustainable funds with lower rating over the 2005–2008 period—the period around the financial crisis. Similarly, sustainable funds perform better after the financial crisis and do not seem affected by the diversification cost, which the authors claim might be offset by the benefits from being classified and perceived as sustainable (Becchetti et al., 2015).

For what concerns the comparison with conventional funds, (Ter Horst et al., 2011) find that socially responsible funds underperformed conventional funds in many European and Asia–Pacific countries in terms of risk-adjusted returns by up to 5% yearly, apart from the United States and the United Kingdom where the performance of these two categories is statistically undistinguishable. The dataset uses mutual fund data (463 funds) from 23 different countries all over the world over the period January 1991–December 2003.

On the other hand, Becchetti et al. (2015) focus on all equity investment funds included in the Morningstar database in the period 1992–2012 and find that sustainable investment funds do not outperform or underperform conventional ones, with some time segments favoring the former and others favoring the latter in terms of risk-adjusted returns.

investment category is selected for inclusion; voting and engagement, whereby companies are selected voting upon them in terms of their ESG scores; ESG integration, whereby ESG risks are included directly in the evaluation of companies; impact investing, whereby sustainable companies are chosen and invested upon in order to pursue sustainability goals in addition to financial returns; norm-based screening, whereby investment products are screened on the basis of compliance with specific rules; and sustainability-themed, whereby financial products chosen need to focus on a specific ESG objective targeted to sustainability. (Retrieved at https://www.eurosif.org/responsible-investment-strategies/).

Bodhanwala and Bodhanwala (2020) use a broad definition of sustainable investment and look at Thomson Reuters' corporate responsibility ratings to select the most sustainable firms in seven geographical areas including developed (United States, United Kingdom, and Australia) and developing nations (Brazil, China, India, and Russia). Instead of using sustainable mutual funds, the authors selected stocks for companies with an ESG Thomson Reuters rating in the top 20% of the rating distribution for each country in 2015. Portfolios were constructed and their performance over the 2009–2015 timeframe was analyzed in comparison with country-specific benchmark indices.[15] The comparisons show that sustainable investment underperforms compared to the benchmark in developing countries, but overperforms in developed ones. The small sample size of sustainable companies in developing countries due to the basic lack of stringent ESG regulation is to blame for this discrepancy according to the authors and indirectly testifies to the role of regulation in creating profitable market opportunities.

Going back to Das et al. (2018) the comparison with the US market performance shows that sustainable funds tend to show lower risk-adjusted returns, a fact that the authors expected and justify by claiming that beating the market is unlikely to be a concern of sustainable investors.

Friede et al. (2015) take a wider perspective in analyzing the relationship between sustainable investing and corporate financial performance (CFP) running a second-order meta-study reviewing over 2000 individual papers gathered through 35 vote-count studies and 25 meta studies.[16] CFP dimensions analyzed in these papers go beyond simple portfolio performance, but include also "accounting-based performance, market-based performance, operational performance, perceptual performance, growth metrics, risk measures" (ibid, p. 4). The interesting result of this

[15] The benchmark indices used are Standard & Poor's 500 composite price index for the sustainable US-stock portfolio; FTSE100 for the sustainable UK-stock portfolio S&P/ASX 200 index for the Australian sustainable portfolio; Standard & Poor's Bombay Stock Exchange-Sensex for the Indian sustainable stock portfolio; Bovespa total return index for the Brazilian case, MICEX index for the Russian one and the Shanghai composite index for the Chinese sustainable stock portfolio.

[16] Vote-count studies and meta studies are two very different methodologies: this implies that only 12% of the papers used in these two groups overlap. Vote-count studies are less sophisticated meta-analysis, where the authors count the number of studies with significant positive, negative, and nonsignificant results and the category with the highest share is voted as winner.

study is that when one looks more holistically at the impact of sustainability on CFP most studies find a nonnegative relationship between ESG factors and CFP. Only when the analysis is run on portfolio-based studies only the positive relationship disappears and the more usual negative impact between ESG and CFP appears again.

The previous section on the comprehensive package of measures that is being implemented in the European Union has shown that sustainability should permeate all levels of corporate life, with sustainable financial products as the key means to re-orient financial flows toward more sustainable corporations. Looking more holistically at how being compliant with ESG demands impacts the overall corporate financial performance appears as a good way to pave the way for this holistic transformation of the European Union.

2.2.3 Social Reasons

A relatively rich strand of literature focuses on the possibility that sustainable investors derive more than mere financial returns from investing in sustainable companies. This idea can be broadly summarized using the term social preferences and implies that individuals may draw some form of satisfaction simply from holding sustainable investments or from letting other people know about them. Social preferences are not tied to financial considerations and bring a different form of utility to the individuals, but how to compose material (financial) and immaterial (social) preferences is not straightforward for individuals, especially when it comes to regulating and performing fiduciary duties in doing so.

Puaschunder (2017) distinguishes different types of social preferences; even if a proper discussion of social preferences is beyond the scope of this book, it is important to at least provide some basic definitions and implications. A very important one is altruism, through which individuals increase the well-being of others through their choices/actions and may derive short-term gratification (warm glow) from the altruistic act. Altruism may be motivated by other-regarding preferences and for the sustainable investor maps into being willing to receive lower returns in exchange for investing in activities that (also) benefit others. Another social driver of sustainable investment is the desire to support and spur sustainable innovation: only by supporting companies that push the edge of the current economic-performance paradigm a real shift can be achieved.

The relevance of social, non-material considerations behind the sustainable investment is that the possibility to align one's behavior with moral preferences might help cushion the disappointment felt when one's moral investment turns out not performing as well as was expected (Rubaltelli et al., 2015).

Several papers provide empirical tests of the different motives for sustainable investment in different domains and using a plurality of tools (survey, fund/portfolio flows, hypothetical scenarios, and incentivized economic experiments). The first important domain to test the role of social preferences is **pension funds**, which represent an ideal domain to test the tension between fulfilling material and immaterial goals. On one side, pension fund's clients have no say in the fund's asset composition; this generates on the fund's side a fiduciary duty to select the financial products that are more likely to produce the best possible financial result to protect the financial well-being of fund holders. On the other hand, preferences for sustainability might pursue a different kind of satisfaction while at the same time hinder the pursuit of the fiduciary duty just expressed.

Borgers and Pownall (2014) look at field data of a representative sample of Dutch households[17] collected in the first quarter of 2011 targeted to shed light on environmental and social preferences of the general public. The survey is framed in the pension-fund domain and requires participant to state their preferences for different investment screens to be applied in the investment fund. Participants are then asked to provide their willingness to pay for the personalization of the investment strategy to include the different screens. This allows to test at the same time which, if any, positive social utility participants get from the investment being sustainable and whether individuals can compose material and immaterial preferences. In principle this type of personalization would not be possible in an investment fund, but if individuals were able to combine the (material) disutility from having to pay for the sustainable personalization with the (immaterial) utility from being a sustainable investor, this would call for assessing sustainability preferences and allowing clients to determine the investment strategy. One limitation to this potential development is whether individuals are sufficiently skilled to do so, and which are the factors that make them more likely to

[17] The final participant pool includes 1176 members of Dutch households aged 20 or more.

be. The paper shows that individuals are willing to pay for their preferred screens in principle but when trying to implement this strategy they have a hard time translating preferences into economically rational behavior: for instance, some state a positive willingness to pay but declare no preference for the screened portfolio or state different desired stock levels for screened and non-screened portfolios that do not reflect their stated preferences. Given the fact that the subject pool is not very financially literate, the authors consider that low financial literacy is likely to determine this inability to compose material and immaterial utility considerations.

Remaining in the pension-fund domain, the idea that the choice to be sustainable produces a boost in satisfaction is found also in (Bauer et al., 2021), who present a study comprising of two surveys where real pension-fund subscribers were involved in the decision to tilt the fund's investment choices more toward sustainability issues (survey 1) and were later asked to report their support for the implemented change (survey 2). The study, despite acknowledging the lack of representative sample, presents some interesting conclusions because it shows that even if investors were warned that a stronger focus on sustainability was not likely to immediately translate into increased returns, most participants supported the move (67.9%) and continued to do so overwhelmingly (98% of those who supported the move in the first survey and participated in the second one) when asked two years later if they were still convinced about the validity of their choice. Financial preferences or social preferences for sustainability might have explained this choice, but the authors prove that financial motives do not matter much: 58% of those who think that sustainable investments lead to lower financial returns still support the move to tilt the pension fund's portfolio more toward sustainability. The relevance of this study lies also in its real consequences: the pension fund was openly committed to adhering to the majority vote of its subscribers in terms of increasing the sustainability share of the investments (which they indeed did), and this new investment strategy mapped into real pensions premia for the participants, making the stakes very salient.

Another interesting study bridging different types of data looks at social preferences of real investors by directly comparing conventional and sustainable options (Riedl & Smeets, 2017). The authors combine administrative data from a Dutch mutual fund provider selling both sustainable and conventional funds over the June 2006–June 2012 period, survey questions and behavior in an incentivized economic experiment to create a more complex picture of the implications and motivation for sustainability preferences. Looking at the data and the survey questions, it is remarkable that risk perceptions[18] are not related in a statistically significant way to choosing a sustainable funds, although larger portfolios[19] with longer investment horizons have more of them (maybe for diversification reasons). Moreover, socially responsible investors are more pessimistic about the expected returns of sustainable funds compared to conventional investors, but the data show that from a statistical perspective the financial performance of sustainable and conventional equity funds is not consistently different over the time frame, although at individual level the mean returns of the sustainable component of the portfolio underperforms compared to the conventional one and determines higher fees. Given these results, the authors conclude that social motives are more likely to play a role. While survey questions explore preferences regarding investment goals and attitudes toward sustainable investment in terms of expected risks and returns, a trust game[20] is used to measure social preferences, focusing on the amount transferred back from the second player to the first: a selfish individual would not transfer any money, while any positive transfer indicates some degree of other-regarding preferences. Since choosing sustainable investment might lead to lower returns, the authors claim that giving up some endowment to a stranger in an anonymous, one-shot trust game might be a good proxy of why individuals choose to invest sustainably. The anonymity and lack of repetition of the game also ensure that no reputation considerations are at play. Even though only 16% of the sample holds a sustainable funds,[21] those who split equally the money in the trust game are 14% more likely to invest sustainably. Moreover, individuals with stronger social preferences invest more in sustainable funds, but even those with

[18] Elicited via an incentivized multiple price list lotteries similar to (Holt & Laury, 2002).

[19] Portfolio size is the only significant difference in terms of portfolio characteristics.

[20] A trust game (Berg et al., 1995) is a simple two-person game, where an amount of money is transferred from one player to the other and then back to the first one. The experiment normally increases the value of the transfer from player 1 to 2 by a factor 3. The game has stark economic predictions: selfish individuals would not transfer anything (nor as players 1 or 2), while it is socially optimum to transfer everything as player 1. Any positive transfer from 1 to 2 and back testifies of some form of social preferences. The Trust Game is a very popular economic game that has been replicated and studied extensively, for a review see (Johnson & Mislin, 2011).

[21] The paper defines sustainable investors those who hold at least one sustainable fund.

weak social preferences chose some sustainable investment if they also have a strong preference for signaling to others that they are sustainable investors. This proves that social signaling might tilt even selfish individuals to engage in sustainable investment. Further analyses explore whether specific demographics are more likely to describe an investor with strong social preferences or with a strong preference for signaling; the results do not show one gender or age as being more prosocial, which suggests that measuring social preference cannot be done indirectly through any of these variables. On the contrary, young, male investors are more prone to social signaling, as are individuals that do not hold a University degree.

The role of social preferences toward sustainable investment can also be found in (Hartzmark & Sussman, 2019), who exploit a natural experiment to show that sustainability ratings drive investment choices in the US mutual fund industry. Since 2016 Morningstar started publicly reported sustainability ratings of mutual funds using a 1-to-5 globe rating; empirical evidence shows that significant flows went toward the 5-globe rated products at the expense of 1-globe rated ones, with minor differences among the other categories. In particular, the authors estimate that in the 11 months after the ratings' publication 1-globe funds lost 12–15 million dollars while 5-globe funds gained 24–25 million dollars in assets. Moreover, what matters most is the globe rating: even if sustainability ratings are available within each category, they do not drive major differences, suggesting that investors tend to focus on the synthetic rating more than on detailed information about the sustainability strategy. In a complement to this analysis, a survey was run with MBA students and Amazon Turk workers to elicit risk and return expectations of the different globe-rated funds. The results show that there exists a strong positive relation between ratings and expected return but a strong negative relation between ratings and expected risk. This inverse relation between risk and return is consistent with the affect heuristic (Slovic et al., 2007), whereby risk perceptions are altered by the presence of an affective relation toward the problem. Individuals who feel more strongly about social and environmental preferences are likely to see higher benefits and lower risks compared to what would be rational to expect. The difference in the amount of money allocated to 5-globe versus 1-globe funds in the experiments cannot be explained simply by risk-returns expectations neither for MBA nor for M-turkers, suggesting that non-material motives regarding the added value of being sustainable exist.[22]

Gutsche and Ziegler (2019) look at a series of stated-choice (SC) experiments[23] using a representative sample of the German population (1001 participants in an online survey) to determine the willingness to pay for different sustainability features in financial products. The financial products included in the SC experiments include some features that are not currently available in the market but have been devised with the help of market practitioners in order to increase the external validity of the experiment. The first experiment deals with a fixed-interest product while the second with an equity fund and participants are required to express their preferences for some pecuniary characteristics of both. More importantly, participants also needed to state their interest toward sustainability criteria, their perception regarding the riskiness of sustainability products, their agreement with the fact that investing sustainably makes one feel good (a warm glow motive), the expectations felt from the social environment to invest sustainably, environmental values and political orientation and some socio-demographic variables (gender, age, education, being married and living in West Germany). Results show that participants exhibit a strong preference for sustainability coupled with a higher willingness to pay for more sustainable products. Respondents that declare to have a left-wing political orientation, belong to environmental groups, and that are susceptible to warm glow display a significantly higher willingness to pay than the other groups. Social considerations are not alone in explaining preferences for sustainability, as individuals who perceive sustainable equity investment as less or equally risky than conventional investment tend to display a higher stated preference for sustainability, which suggest that risk considerations do have a place when dealing with sustainable investment processes. This paper suggests that some social

[22] This effect is stronger for individuals who confirm to having taken sustainability considerations in mind when making the allocation, although more so for Turkers than MBA students.

[23] This type of data is collected in survey where individuals make choices over hypothetical scenarios; one advantage of this type of data is that individuals might be exposed to experiences or situations that currently are not available to them. On the other hand, the hypothetical nature of the decisions might give rise to hypothetical biases and reduced external validity.

motives are the dimensions more likely to make investors want to part with some expected return to ensure that their investment choices are sustainable.

2.3 Are Sustainable Investors Biased?

Economic motives seem to be just one of the determinants of the choice to invest sustainably and the previous section has highlighted in which directions real sustainable investors stray away from conventional economic reasoning: social motives, other-regarding preferences, and emotional considerations all seem to play a role when sustainable investment is considered. Another dimension to discuss to conclude our overview of the features of the sustainable investor explores if sustainable investors are more prone to boundedly rational behavior than conventional investors and if so, how. These questions are crucial to understand if the assumptions of the traditional asset-pricing and financial decision models that are used to decide and affect portfolio allocations are actually met by the real investors.

Behavioral finance looks at how individuals use decision processes that are alternative to the classic paradigms of economic rationality; real investors are not characterized by complete oversight, have not use for perfect information since then to be prone to cognitive overload and use shortcuts in behavior (heuristics, as defined for instance in the large program initiated by Kahneman and Tversky at the end of the 1970s) to help them navigate the complex and uncertain world of financial investment. A review of the key tenets of behavioral finance is not necessary to understand the behavioral implications of sustainable investment[24]; it is important to highlight that behavioral finance allows to both shed light on individual determinants and look at how such individual tendencies map onto the aggregate market behavior. The literature on the role of behavioral biases in sustainable investment is not currently very rich, but we can find some interesting patterns that deserve mention insofar as their implications for financial advisory and the definition of a portfolio allocation that truly reflects investors' characteristics. We look at biases dealing with updating information and the role of the past; the disposition effect and emotions.

[24] For a short and effective review see for instance (Barberis & Thaler, 2003).

2.3.1 Updating Information and the Role of the Past

The rational economic decision-maker is supposed to be incorporating new information into the old one using Bayesian updating. Several experiments and empirical analysis with probability estimations and updating have shown that the general person is not very good at applying Bayesian updating. Individuals tend to attach layers of meaning to new information, sometimes overstating its importance and content, and sometimes neglecting it. This pattern is at the basis of the three seminal heuristics defined by Kahneman and Tversky: representativeness, availability, and anchoring[25] (Kahneman et al., 1982). These individual biases have several notable impacts in financial behavior both at individual and at aggregate level. For instance, representativeness can explain momentum and anchoring explains underreaction to new information. Although a clear connection between seminal biases and sustainable investment has not yet been established in the literature, there are some patterns regarding sustainable funds' past performance and their impact on current investors' choices that suggest that they might have a role. Bollen (2007) looks at volatility and performance of socially responsible funds in comparison with conventional ones and finds that cash flows into sustainable funds are more stable (have lower volatility) and that sustainable investors are more sensitive to lagged positive returns than conventional ones, but less sensitive to negative returns. These patterns are explained by the preference for holding sustainable funds, ranging from mature to newer funds in mostly the same way. Moreover, these patterns are robust and persistent in time. Renneboog et al. (2011) further explore them focusing exclusively on sustainable funds and using an international database of screened funds

[25] Representativeness generally implies that individuals weight information based on similarity with the features of the population: a sample that looks more coherent with the general features of the universe it is drawn from is considered more likely. It maps into overweighting new information and disregarding the stream of accumulated knowledge. Thus a very positive stock-market result might be seen as representative of the future of the stock, generating momentum, for which stock performance continues to be positively autocorrelated (until possibly, irrational expectations are reversed, and the price reverts to fundamentals). Availability is another instance of overweighting new information over older one but is normally due to salience or relevance of the new information; it explains why attention-grabbing events have an impact on stock price movements. Anchoring, on the other hand, is the tendency to anchor to past information and disregard new ones and explains why sometimes prices exhibit a slow process of incorporating new information (e.g., earnings announcements) generating underreaction to new information.

and confirm that sustainable investors are less affected by past performance than conventional ones. How they are more positively affected in the event of positive performance also depends on the screen used in the fund, with social screens being less effective than environmental ones in generating a positive response in sustainable investors. The authors also find that there is no smart-money effect: the funds that receive more funds do neither outperform nor underperform funds that receive smaller inflows.

2.3.2 *The Disposition Effect and Emotions*

The disposition effect (Odean, 1998; Shefrin & Statman, 1985) implies that investors tend to sell stocks that are gaining value faster than they sell stocks that are losing; this behavior is not rational, as the mere implications that stock price losses can be used for reducing tax liabilities should push a rational investor to sell losers faster than winners. Other rational explanations such as private information, speculation, and transaction costs are also ruled out in empirical analysis (Odean, 1998). In this seminal article, Shefrin and Statman show that this effect is especially strong throughout the year except in the month of December (when the tax-loss selling pressure is stronger) and provide two related behavioral explanations for it. The first one combines mental accounting (Thaler, 2008) with the implications of prospect theory (Kahneman & Tversky, 1979; Tversky & Kahneman, 1992). Mental accounting refers to the tendency of keeping separate accounts for different types of expenses; thus, each stock has its own account, where price increases and decreases are recorded. Mental accounts are opened at purchase and closed only when the asset is sold. Prospect theory is a remarkable descriptive theory of behavior that has been developed from significant amounts of empirical evidence, whose key message is that risk propensities vary across different domains: people tend to be risk averse in the domain of gains (but risk loving when the probability of a gain is very small) and risk loving in the domain of losses (being risk averse when the probability of the loss is also very small). Besides describing reversed attitudes across the two domains, the PT value function has two more notable features: the convex trait over losses is steeper than the concave trait in the domain of gains, which implies that losses loom larger than gains—almost twice as much! Moreover, probabilities are not considered by individuals at face value but are weighted through an S-shaped weighting function. Combining mental accounting and prospect theory helps explaining the disposition effect as follows. Individuals keep track of individual stock performances and when a stock is losing value feel in the domain of losses; the loss is only a paper loss until the stock is sold thus, they refrain from selling also because, feeling the looming loss they become more risk seeking and prefer to hold on to the stock hoping for a change of fortune. The disposition effect might also be explained using an emotional framework that builds on this first explanation: selling the losing stock (and closing the account) certifies that a bad decision (the purchase of the stock) was made, while cashing in on the extra profits selling the winning one is a source of pride. Individuals feel regret much strongly and want to avoid it, thus holding on to the losing stocks.

The disposition effect (DE) has been documented in a variety of time frames and markets, but the literature on individual determinants is not very large as most studies focus on market-level analysis that prevents from understanding properly individual motives even if investors are financially hurt in the process, as winners sold outperform losers held by 3.41% on a risk-adjusted basis (Odean, 1998). Kaustia (2010) reviews several empirical evidence on the determinants of the DE and highlights its relevance across very different financial actors. Shapira and Venezia (2001) find that investors aided by a financial advisors seem to be less prone to the DE. Da Costa et al. (2013) focus on the role of investor experience in mitigating the DE building on the mixed results from stock-market studies (supporting the positive role of experience) and laboratory studies (disproving it) and find, using a computerized experiment simulating the stock market with two samples of experienced (real stock investors with a minimum 2-year experience) and inexperienced traders (students) that experience (if over 5 years) matters in reducing this bias. Cecchini et al. (2019) present an individual-level analysis that looks at the role of personality traits and finds, using economic experiments with students in Italy and China, that extroverts are more prone to the disposition effect due to their higher sensitivity to rewards, while individuals high in conscientiousness and openness to experiences result much less biased. Conscientious individuals can resist the urge to capitalize on gains quickly and are able to factor in and process this information to devise more successful trading strategies.

The DE has also been studied in relation to sustainable investment. van Dooren and Galema (2018) develop an individual-level analysis of real portfolios from retail investors of a large multinational retail bank from the Netherlands including all trades in 2015 (December excluded) and compare the behavior of sustainable investors (defined as investors that only hold socially responsible stocks) with other conventional investors.[26] No financial advisors are involved in the decisions, as clients manage their portfolios on their own, which allows to use portfolio decision to identify the DE, and information about clients and the stocks traded to make inferences on the reasons for the presence or absence of this effect. The data show that although the DE is present among investors, its effect is stronger for sustainable investors (19% of the trades compared to 11% when looking at the whole sample) and statistically different than that of conventional investors (7.9% higher than them). Investor sophistication and trading experience mitigate the DE and so do wealth and age. The investors in the sample are characterized by different levels of investment in sustainable stocks: when looking at the relationship between how much is allocated to such stocks and the DE the authors find that only for investors that allocate at least 85% of their portfolio to sustainable stocks the DE increases with the share allocated to such activities, but for lower values there exist no significant relationship between DE and share of funds allocated to sustainable investment.

Given the relevance of emotional considerations for the DE, we conclude this tour of the potential impact of biases by focusing on affective reactions. Rubaltelli et al. (2010) test whether affective reactions impact the selling prices of a stock that is losing value in an experimental design featuring two funds to evaluate. Both funds are described with identical fundamentals but only one is framed as socially responsible. Participants were required to set the selling price for the stocks assuming they were losing money. Empirical findings show that stocks belonging to industries that are described as socially responsible trigger more positive affective reactions and reach higher selling prices. Thus, affective reactions in a sense "locked" individuals into the losing funds, emphasizing a pattern that is similar to the one observed in the disposition effect and making them unable to sell the losing fund as quickly as people with negative feelings.

[26] There are 6924 investors in the dataset, 1717 of whom are investing exclusively in sustainable stocks.

3 Implications for Financial Risk Tolerance and Investment Choices

The challenge to shift investment flows toward sustainability is just the last page of a complex history where academic research, regulation, and stakeholders' feedback shape the boundaries of what individuals and institution can and should do when investing. Just like the introduction of the suitability questionnaire with MiFID has provided a general framework to ensure investment effectiveness and coherence with investment goals, MiFID2 has shifted the focus on investor protection introducing more stringent informational requirements in terms of information flows and introduced considerations rooted in behavioral theories like the ability to bear losses. The challenge to introduce sustainability preferences within the suitability questionnaire in an effective way is the most obvious challenge facing market players at the moment and we have discussed how this step affects also several other actions in the Action Plan. Only if individual investors truly prefer the sustainable product, the increased costs for improved and transparent corporate processes and sustainability disclosure will pay off for firms.

The long journey undertaken in this chapter was aimed at highlighting some important points in the implementation of the European vision for a sustainable finance. First of all, while there is significant appetite for sustainable products, current suggestions regarding the assessment of sustainability preferences do not include factors that theoretical and empirical evidence have shown to be important like social preferences, altruism, or the desire for social signaling. All these processes have been documented in the literature and several simple tools exist to measure them.

Secondly, but not less importantly, sustainability and risk behavior are considered two separate avenues, with sustainability assessed on top of the other risk-related dimensions according to the indications of the European Commission and ESMA. The analysis of the empirical literature has shown that the sustainable investor is more prone to biases that have a lot to do with risk and with losses, which suggests that a feedback loop between risk and sustainability preferences might have been overlooked.

While the exploration of these concerns will require more empirical research, another possible challenge to the pursuit of investor protection is taking center stage: the increasing diffusion of technology is starting to offer financial markets interesting opportunities for fintech applications. The next chapter will look more closely at how this other important change might represent an opportunity and not only a challenge.

References

Barberis, N., & Thaler, R. (2003). A survey of behavioral finance. *Handbook of the Economic of Finance, 1*, 1053–1128. https://doi.org/10.2139/ssrn.327880

Bauer, R., Ruof, T., & Smeets, P. (2021). Get real! Individuals prefer more sustainable investments. *Review of Financial Studies, 34*(8), 3976–4043. https://doi.org/10.1093/rfs/hhab037

Becchetti, L., Ciciretti, R., Dalò, A., & Herzel, S. (2015). Socially responsible and conventional investment funds: Performance comparison and the global financial crisis. *Applied Economics, 47*(25), 2541–2562. https://doi.org/10.1080/00036846.2014.1000517

Berg, J., Dickhaut, J., & McCabe, K. (1995). Trust reciprocity and social history. *Games and Economic Behavior, 10*, 122–142. https://doi.org/10.1006/game.1995.1027

Bodhanwala, S., & Bodhanwala, R. (2020). Relationship between sustainable and responsible investing and returns: A global evidence. *Social Responsibility Journal, 16*(4), 579–594. https://doi.org/10.1108/SRJ-12-2018-0332

Bollen, N. P. B. (2007). Mutual fund attributes and investor behavior. *The Journal of Financial and Quantitative Analysis, 42*(3), 683–708.

Borgers, A. C. T., & Pownall, R. A. J. (2014). Attitudes towards socially and environmentally responsible investment. *Journal of Behavioral and Experimental Finance, 1*, 27–44. https://doi.org/10.1016/j.jbef.2014.01.005

Cecchini, M., Bajo, E., Russo, P. M., & Sobrero, M. (2019). Individual differences in the disposition effect. *Journal of Behavioral Finance, 20*(1), 107–126. https://doi.org/10.1080/15427560.2018.1492579

Council of the European Union. (2016). European Benchmark Regulation. *Official Journal of the European Union, 59*.

Da Costa, N., Goulart, M., Cupertino, C., Macedo, J., & Da Silva, S. (2013). The disposition effect and investor experience. *Journal of Banking and Finance, 37*(5), 1669–1675. https://doi.org/10.1016/j.jbankfin.2012.12.007

Das, N., Chatterje, S., Ruf, B., & Sunder, A. (2018). ESG ratings and the performance of socially responsible mutual funds: A panel study. *Journal of Finance Issues, 17*(1), 49–57.

EBA. (2019, December). *EBA Action Plan*.

ERM. (2020). *Study on sustainability-related ratings, data and research*. https://op.europa.eu/en/publication-detail/-/publication/897bee11-509d-11eb-b59f-01aa75ed71a1

ESA. (2021). Final report on draft regulatory technical standards. *Joint Committee Of The European Supervisory Authoroties*, *JC*(2021 03).

ESA. (2022). *Clarifications on the ESA's draft RTS under SFDR* (Issue June).

EU High-Level Expert Group on Sustainable Finance. (2018). Financing a sustainable European economy. In *European Commission* (Issue January). https://ec.europa.eu/info/sites/info/files/180131-sustainable-finance-final-report_en.pdf

European Commission. (2018). Action plan: Financing sustainable growth. *EUR-Lex*, 20. https://eur-lex.europa.eu/legal-content/EN/TXT/?uri=CELEX:52018DC0097

European Commission. (2019a). *Commision Delegated regulation (EU) 2021/1257 of 21 April 2021 amending Delegated Regulation (EU) 2017/2358 and Delegated Regulation (EU) 2017/2359 as regards the integration of sustainability factors and preferences into the product oversight and governance requirements for insurance undertakings and insurance distributors and into the rules on conduct of business and investment advice for insurance-based investment products*. https://eur-lex.europa.eu/legal-content/EN/TXT/?uri=CELEX%3A32021R1257

European Commission. (2019b). The European green deal—communication from the commission to the European parliament, the European council, the council, the European economic and social committee and the committee of the regions. In *Introduction to Knowledge Management* (pp. 106–117). https://doi.org/10.4324/9780080495781-12

European Commission. (2020a). *Stepping up Europe's 2030 climate ambition Investing in a climate-neutral future for the benefit of our people* (Vol. 53, Issue 9, pp. 1689–1699). https://knowledge4policy.ec.europa.eu/publication/communication-com2020562-stepping-europe%E2%80%99s-2030-climate-ambition-investing-climate_en#:~:text=17%20September%202020-,Communication%20COM%2F2020%2F562%3A%20Stepping%20up%20Europe's%202030%20climate,the%20benefit%20of%20our%20people&text=With%20the%202030%20Climate%20Target,below%201990%20levels%20by%202030

European Commission. (2020b). *Summary report on the public consultation on the Evaluation and Review of the Non-Financial Reporting Directive. February*, 5–7. https://ec.europa.eu/digital-single-market/en/news/summary-report-public-consultation-evaluation-and-review-eprivacy-directive

European Commission. (2021a). *Commission Delegated Regulation (EU) 2021/2178*, *2016*(68), 48–119.

European Commission. (2021b). *Commission delegated regulation amending Delegated Regulation (EU) 2017/565 as regards the integration of sustainability factors, risks and preferences into certain organisational requirements and operating conditions for investment firms* (Vol. 1, Issue 69, pp. 5–24).
European Commission. (2021c). *Proposal for Regulation of the European Parliament and of the Council on European green bonds, 0191*(July), 1–23.
European Parliament. (2019). Regulation (EU) 2019/2089 of the European Parliament as regards EU Climate Transition Benchmarks, EU Paris-aligned Benchmarks and sustainability-related disclosures for benchmarks. *Official Journal of the European Union, December* (November), 17–27.
European Parliament and the Council. (2020). Regulation (EU) 2020/852 of 18 June 2020 on the establishment of a framework to facilitate sustainable investment, and amending Regulation (EU) 2019/2088. *Official Journal of the European Union, 2019*(October 2016), 13–43.
European Securities and Markets Authority. (2019, April). ESMA's technical advice to the European Commission on integrating sustainability risks and factors in MiFID II. *European Securities and Markets Authority.*
European Securities and Markets Authority. (2022, January). *Consultation Paper Guidelines on certain aspects of the MiFID II suitability requirements.* www.esma.europa.eu
Fleming, R. C., & Mauger, R. (2021). Green and just? An update on the "European green deal." *Journal for European Environmental and Planning Law, 18*(1), 164–180. https://doi.org/10.1163/18760104-18010010
Friede, G., Busch, T., & Bassen, A. (2015). ESG and financial performance: Aggregated evidence from more than 2000 empirical studies. *Journal of Sustainable Finance and Investment, 5*(4), 210–233. https://doi.org/10.1080/20430795.2015.1118917
Gutsche, G., & Ziegler, A. (2019). Which private investors are willing to pay for sustainable investments? Empirical evidence from stated choice experiments. *Journal of Banking and Finance, 102*, 193–214. https://doi.org/10.1016/j.jbankfin.2019.03.007
Hartzmark, S. M., & Sussman, A. B. (2019). Do investors value sustainability? A natural experiment examining ranking and fund flows. *Journal of Finance, 74*(6), 2789–2837. https://doi.org/10.1111/jofi.12841
Hayes, J. (2001). The greater good: How ethical investment pays off. *Australian Financial Review, 26*(8), 29–31.
Holt, C. A., & Laury, S. K. (2002). Risk aversion and incentive effects. *The American Economic Review, 92*(5), 1644–1655. https://www.jstor.org/stable/3083270
Johnson, N. D., & Mislin, A. A. (2011). Trust games: A meta-analysis. *Journal of Economic Psychology, 32*(5), 865–889. https://doi.org/10.1016/j.joep.2011.05.007

Kahneman, D., Slovic, P., & Tversky, A. (1982). *Judgement under uncertainty: Heuristics and biases*. Cambridge University Press.

Kahneman, D., & Tversky, A. (1979). Prospect theory: An analysis of decision under risk. *Econometrica: Journal of the Econometric Society*, *47*(3), 263–291. https://doi.org/10.1111/j.1536-7150.2011.00774.x

Kaustia, M. (2010). Disposition effect. In H. K. Baker & J. R. Nofsinger (Eds.), *Behavioral Finance: Investors, Corporations, and Markets*. John Wiley & Sons, Inc.

Konstantas, A., Faraca, G., Dodd, N., Kofoworola, O., Boyano, A., & Wolf, O. (2021). Development of EU ecolabel criteria for retail financial products—Technical report 2.0: Draft proposal for the product scope and criteria. In *EJRC Technicl Reports* (Issue March). https://www.cric-online.org/images/CRIC/20191220_EU_Ecolabel_FP_Draft_Technical_Report_2-0.pdf

Morgan Stanley Institute for Sustainable Investing. (2019). Sustainable signals. *Institute for Sustainable Investing*, 1–8. https://www.morganstanley.com/pub/content/dam/msdotcom/infographics/sustainable-investing/Sustainable_Signals_Individual_Investor_White_Paper_Final.pdf

Morningstar. (2022a). *Global Sustainable Fund Flows-Q1 2022* (Issue May).

Morningstar. (2022b). *SFDR Article 8 and Article 9 Funds: 2021 in Review*. 1–35. http://global.morningstar.com/equitydisclosures

Odean, T. (1998). Are investors reluctant to realize their losses? *The Journal of Finance*, *53*(5), 1775–1798. http://www.jstor.org/stable/117424

Puaschunder, J. M. (2017). Socio-psychological motives of socially responsible investors. *Advances in Financial Economics, 19*, 209–247. https://doi.org/10.1108/S1569-373220160000019008

Renneboog, L., Ter Horst, J., & Zhang, C. (2011). Is ethical money financially smart? Nonfinancial attributes and money flows of socially responsible investment funds. *Journal of Financial Intermediation, 20*(4), 562–588. https://doi.org/10.1016/j.jfi.2010.12.003

Riedl, A., & Smeets, P. (2017). Why do investors hold socially responsible mutual funds? *Journal of Finance, 72*(6), 2505–2550. https://doi.org/10.1111/jofi.12547

Rosen, B. N., Sandler, D. M., & Shani, D. (1991). Social issues and socially responsibility investment behavior: Preliminary empirical investigation. *Journal of Consumer Affairs, 25*(2), 221–234.

Rubaltelli, E., Lotto, L., Ritov, I., & Rumiati, R. (2015). Moral investing: Psychological motivations and implications. *Judgment and Decision Making*, *10*(1), 64–75. http://search.proquest.com/openview/2f74b7e3d679ef0e182c5518f7bc6d96/1?pq-origsite=gscholar%5Cnpapers3://publication/uuid/EBE68E54-1AE3-481D-A7DE-3BCFC899CA2E

Rubaltelli, E., Pasini, G., Rumiati, R., Olsen, R. A., & Slovic, P. (2010). The influence of affective reactions on investment decisions. *Journal of Behavioral Finance, 11*(3), 168–176. https://doi.org/10.1080/15427560.2010.507409

Shapira, Z., & Venezia, I. (2001). Patterns of behavior of professionally managed and independent investors. *Journal of Banking and Finance, 25*(8), 1573–1587. https://doi.org/10.1016/S0378-4266(00)00139-4

Shefrin, H., & Statman, M. (1985). The disposition to sell winners too early and ride losers too long: theory and evidence. *The Journal of Finance*, *40*(3).

Slovic, P., Finucane, M. L., Peters, E., & MacGregor, D. G. (2007). The affect heuristic. *European Journal of Operational Research, 177*(3), 1333–1352. https://doi.org/10.1016/j.ejor.2005.04.006

Sparkes, R. (2002). *Socially responsible investment: A global revolution*. Wiley.

Ter Horst, J. R., Zhang, C., & Renneboog, L. (2011). The price of ethics: Evidence from socially responsible mutual funds. *SSRN Electronic Journal*. https://doi.org/10.2139/ssrn.985265

Thaler, R. H. (2008). Mental accounting and consumer choice. *Marketing Science, 27*(1), 15–25. https://doi.org/10.1287/mksc.l070.0330

The European Parliament and the Council. (2019). Regulation (EU) 2019/2088 of the European parliament and of the council on sustainability-related disclosures in the financial services sector. *Official Journal of the EU*, *2019*(April), 1–16. https://eur-lex.europa.eu/legal-content/EN/TXT/PDF/?uri=CELEX:32019R2088&from=EN

Tversky, A., & Kahneman, D. (1992). Advances in prospect-theory—cumulative representation of uncertainty. *Journal of Risk and Uncertainty*, *5*(4), 297–323. https://doi.org/10.1007/Bf00122574

van Dooren, B., & Galema, R. (2018). Socially responsible investors and the disposition effect. *Journal of Behavioral and Experimental Finance, 17*, 42–52. https://doi.org/10.1016/j.jbef.2017.12.006

CHAPTER 4

The Digital Challenge: How Are New Technologies Shaping the Financial Industry?

Abstract This chapter describes the challenges that the digitalization of the financial services industries is posing to traditional players. In particular, the Fintech revolution, Open Banking/Finance, and robo advisory are described, both on a practical and academic ground, focusing on how the transition from in-person financial services to automated ones affects the trust paradigm and, eventually, investors' risk tolerance. The chapter also recaps the Payment Services Directive 2 and the role played by the European Regulator in contributing to the dissemination of digital solutions, instilling confidence in the use of digital services, and facilitating and encouraging competition in the finance industry. The chapter concludes with the revised Guidelines on Suitability issued by ESMA in 2018, where new requirements have been introduced to consider the increasing presence of robo advisors in the market for financial advice.

Keywords Technology · Fintech · Robo advisory · Trust in automation · Suitability

© The Author(s), under exclusive license to Springer Nature Switzerland AG 2022

C. Cruciani et al., *Understanding Financial Risk Tolerance*,
https://doi.org/10.1007/978-3-031-13131-8_4

1 The Technological Revolution of the Financial Services Industry

1.1 The Digitalization and Open Challenges

The 2008 financial crisis paved the way for financial technology (Fintech) and financial digitalization, completely undermining competition within the financial services industry and strongly affecting individuals' attitudes and behavior in financial decision-making, thanks to the higher cost-efficiency and accessibility of these financial services and products. The (World Economic Forum, 2015) identified financial technology as a disruptive innovation, able to reshape the future of the financial industry and make a significant impact on the functions of financial services, including payment, insurance, deposits and lending, capital raising, and investment management.

Nowadays, extended competition, Open Banking, APIs, Fintech startups, robo advisory, and process automation, are all pieces of a rich and varied mosaic that the Regulator is guiding, trying to foster competition while preserving the fundamental principles of investor protection and the adequacy and suitability of the products and services offered.

It is, however, clear that moving from traditional in-person financial services to automated ones poses some challenges that are still unresolved regarding the risks that the incumbent banking and advisory models might be likely facing or who are the investors that are more likely to rely on automation and whether their risk tolerance is going to be affected. All these questions are crucial to understand the role of regulation and the possible new normative developments.

The goal of the following paragraphs is threefold: first, to provide the reader with clear definitions of the major financial innovations (particularly, Fintech, Open banking/finance, and robo advisory) and their evolution in the financial industry; secondly, to recall the European regulation regarding the digitization of financial services, which is presumably paving the way for the future MiFID III Directive; and finally to look at the academic perspective, to discover how financial technology is affecting individuals' behavior and risk tolerance, trying to profile the identikit of the "digital investor."

2 Fintech

2.1 A Definition

The term Fintech comes from the contraction of Finance (Fin) and Technology (Tech), to indicate the two strong roots to which it belongs and refers to any use of digital instruments applied in the financial field. At its core, Fintech's purpose is to help companies, business owners, and consumers better manage their financial operations, processes, and lives by utilizing specialized software and algorithms that are used on computers and, increasingly, smartphones. Fintech-Fin startups are focused on one or more financial services and try to optimize them using digital tools; Fintech-Tech startups have a diametrically opposite process in that they start from the development of a specific technology that is then applied to the financial sector.

A more recent evolution of Fintech is the so-called Insurtech, which identifies the entire process of digitalization investing the insurance industry from the underwriting of policies to the management of claims thanks to the use of technologies such as Big Data Analytics, Artificial Intelligence, and APIs.[1]

The areas that Fintech covers can be broadly described as (i) credit deposits, and capital-raising services; (ii) payments, clearing, and settlement services, including digital currencies; (iii) investment management services (including trading); and (iv) Insurance. Part of the technological backbone of Fintech is Blockchain technology.

According to (Thakor, 2020), the use of this technology along with other technological advancements is intended to lower search and verification costs of matching transacting parties, while achieving economies of scale in gathering and using large data and cheaper and more secure information transmission.

Looking at the size of Fintech (Wray et al., 2021) show that the investment waves are hitting a record for Fintech & Insurtech funding, globally reaching around $34.2B (+173% YoY compared to Q3). Americas & Europe, Middle East, and Africa (EMEA) have seen the largest growth in total investment in 2021 Q1–Q3 compared to the same period in 2020, seeing approximately 163% and 155% growth, respectively. The Asia–Pacific area (APAC) has seen the largest growth in investment from

[1] Artificial Programming Interfaces. See following sections for further explanations.

Q2 2021 to Q3 2021, with around \$7 billion raised in 2021 Q3, a 97% growth on that raised in 2021 Q2. Overall, investments in 2021 have experienced substantial growth across all clusters of the Fintech & Insurtech ecosystem but Q3 investments have been notably influenced by Fintech offering Payments and Accounts products, which combined account for about 45% of all investments over the period, claiming \$7.7 billion and \$7.6 billion, respectively.

2.2 *Fintech Users*

There are four broad categories of users for Fintech: business-to-business (B2B) for banks, banks' business clients, business-to-consumer (B2C) for small businesses, and consumers. Trends toward mobile banking, increased information, data, more accurate analytics, and decentralization of access are creating opportunities for all four groups to interact in unprecedented ways.

Looking at the consumers, as with most technology, younger individuals are more likely to be aware of and be able to accurately describe what Fintech is. Consumer-oriented Fintech is mostly targeted toward millennials given the huge size and rising earning (and inheritance) potential of that much-talked-about segment. Some Fintech watchers believe that this focus on millennials has more to do with the size of that marketplace than the ability and interest of Gen Xers and Baby Boomers in using Fintech. Rather, Fintech tends to offer little to older consumers because it fails to address their problems.

When it comes to businesses, before the advent and adoption of Fintech, a business owner or startup would have gone to a bank to secure financing or startup capital. If they intended to accept credit card payments, they would have to establish a relationship with a credit provider and even install infrastructure, such as a landline-connected card reader. Now, with mobile technology, those hurdles are surpassed, and technology is a real opportunity for companies (Fig. 1).

2.3 *Fintech Services*

Fintech services have evolved around different business models (Lee & Shin, 2018), which range from payments to wealth management, from crowdfunding to lending, capital market, and insurance services.

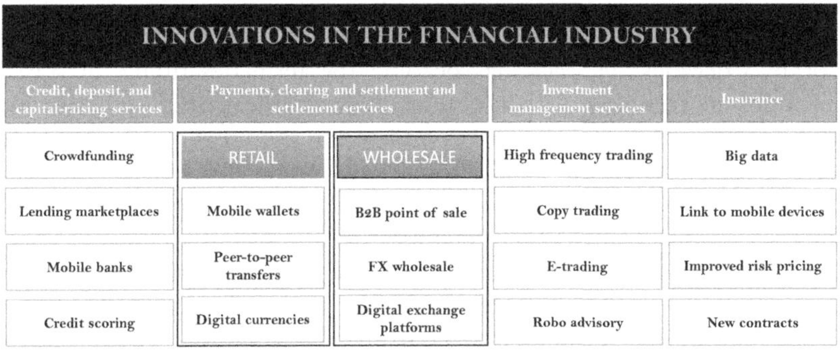

Fig. 1 The four types of financial services that currently are and will be affected by Fintech (*Source* Adapted by [Basel Committee on Banking Supervision, 2018; Thakor, 2020)]

The different aspects of information technology that enable Fintech to change transversally the four types of financial services described above are the following:

- portal and data aggregators;
- ecosystems (to be intended as infrastructure, open-source, APIs[2]);
- data applications (big data analysis, machine learning, predictive modeling);
- distributed ledger technology (blockchain, smart contracts);
- security (customer identification and authentication);
- cloud computing;
- internet of things/mobile technology;
- artificial intelligence (bots, automation in finance, algorithms).

According to a survey conducted by the (Basel Committee on Banking Supervision, 2018), the highest number of Fintech service providers are in payments, clearing, and settlement services, followed by credit, deposit, and capital-raising services.

[2] APIs will be thoroughly described at paragraph 3.1.

2.4 The Academic Point of View on Fintech

For two decades, FinTech has become the term describing all breakthroughs in technology that potentially have the power to transform the provision of financial services and foster the creation of new business models, processes, applications, and products. One of the main concerns of academics is understanding the *risks and opportunities* that FinTech creates for banks and its impact on the main functions of financial intermediaries as well as their role in the modern ecosystems of financial services. (Murinde et al., 2022) systematize this debate and, using high-quality bank-level data from 115 countries worldwide for the past 16 years, compute statistical moments of some key indicators of the changing banking landscape in the FinTech era. Their findings suggest that FinTech lenders are not expected to replace banks, also because banks are developing their FinTech platforms or working with FinTech startups. Focusing on banks' evolution path, it is important to mention the difference between "digitization" and "digitalization": digitization focuses more on the effort to digitize existing processes and tasks (i.e., the move from analog to digital or from a paper-based system to a digital representation of the same data or tasks), while digitalization means moving to a digitally native way of engaging in economic activity that suggests new ways of creating value and the adoption of novel business models, which normally require a more customer-oriented approach (Legner et al., 2017; Tilson et al., 2010). Understandably, the digitization process can do little to keep banks competitive especially toward technology companies and large institutions (i.e., BigTechs), who are seeking to take advantage and enter parts of the finance industry (Shin, 2019). To evolve and remain competitive in the current scenario, the traditional banking industry is expected to face several challenges (Murinde et al., 2022). The first one implies finding new ways of introducing technology in finance. In fact, older technology implementations mainly focused on creating more cost-effective operations to achieve efficiencies through automation, whereas the "new" FinTech is geared toward rethinking entire business processes and introducing new business models in finance. The second is to be careful with "external threats", i.e., entrepreneurs and investors outside financial services (mainly tech firms) ready to take advantage of existing inefficiencies and "disrupt" the status quo. Another challenge involves consumers and implies shifting preferences and demographics of consumers who are becoming more familiar with technology (maybe thanks to their experiences with other high-tech companies, like Google, Spotify, Amazon, Uber, etc.). This type of consumer looks for better, cheaper, and more inclusive products. Despite this, banks are not risking their market share right now and statistics have shown that consumers tend to be "stickier" when it comes to moving bank accounts and using new unfamiliar services by alternative providers (Navaretti et al., 2018). The fourth challenge for traditional banks regards new business models. (Roengpitya et al., 2017; Thakor, 2020) provide an extensive review of current banking business models and how they are at risk. They highlight the multiple-side competition that banks are facing from FinTechs and new digital banks but also entrants from the high-tech industry (producing software or hardware), as well as players from the retail, telecommunications, and other sectors (Dapp et al., 2014). A possible evolution is that a platform business model is established (Murinde et al., 2022), where banks will potentially be the platform provider servicing core functionalities such as customers identity, accounts provision, payments processing, and others while ensuring that there is "order" to the buying and selling of products on their platform. For example, they could play as the guarantor of the quality and seamless integration of the FinTechs that use their platform, making recommendations, and offering services that they could not themselves offer. Of course, APIs open infinite potential evolutions of the role banks can play in this fast-changing environment.

A very crucial challenge for banks is also the *use of data*, on which the future success and survival of the banking institutions will depend. Properly employing data, for example in the areas of fraud, anti-money laundering, and cybersecurity can add immense and often unforeseen benefits to the banking business (Liberti & Petersen, 2019; Puri & Rocholl, 2008). According to (Murinde et al., 2022) banks are also expected to maintain agility and ambidexterity, where ambidexterity is a concept used to describe how an organization needs to be at the intersection between innovation and change (Gupta et al., 2021). According to the prevalent literature, banks have a clear disadvantage against smaller and more agile or "lean" FinTech startups and seasoned high-tech firms. Consequently, they will need to keep a successful balance between maintaining their core capabilities or offerings (i.e., exploiting existing resources), and exploring future opportunities (i.e., leveraging digital innovation and new business models). Banks are also expected to move from a business model based on "selling products" to a new one where they "sell experiences." Digitalization and the extensive use of mobile devices and apps have revolutionized how individuals interact with banks and money. Because of this change in path, banks' challenge will be to expand customers' banking experience. Understandably, this process may also mean a complete overhaul of existing channels, with banks becoming "invisible" and the human interaction set at its minimum (Murinde et al., 2022). The same branches will face a complete redesign to complement digital experiences (i.e., become "phygital" stations), and digital interfaces like chatbots (e.g., conversational AI via audio or text), visual holograms, virtual and augmented reality, will appear more frequently in "places of interest" where customers can be served with easiness.

Another aspect worth to be mentioned is personalization. The massive use of Artificial Intelligence, combined with open APIs, will make the number of "smart banking services" continue growing. A major role in such a context will be played by trust and, in particular, by the ability of banks to protect customers' privacy and personal data. A way of personalizing these new services could not only help track and deliver on user behavior but, occasionally, also nudge (Thaler & Sunstein, 2003) users to make better decisions and enjoy superior outcomes. AI can allow for "nudges" that are tailored to each person and delivered at the right time and place (e.g., interface or application). Finally, banks will have to face the challenge of social responsibility and financial inclusion. Several papers have shown the positive impact of mobile money on financial inclusion. Since technologies help banks reduce the costs of client acquisition, they will have the possibility to reach all categories of customers (disadvantaged or homeless people, immigrants, etc.), thus fostering financial inclusion (Jack & Suri, 2014; Suri & Jack, 2016). Banks are also expected to be more socially responsible concerning climate change, diversity, health, and work–life balance. For example, they can support environmental issues and encourage sustainable behavior, exploiting their digital channels of communication with the customers and even embed some practices in their products (for example, by incorporating recommendations for green investing and ranking opportunities based on carbon emissions data).

3 Open Banking and Open Finance

3.1 A Definition of Open Banking

One example of Open innovation has already been applied within the banking sector and retracing the steps of that experience might help shed light on possible implications for other financial domains and players. Open Banking is the new paradigm according to which financial information and transactions must be freely available to customers without the constraints that currently exist. This new paradigm is changing the competitive logic between banks and financial insurance companies, but at the same time, it affects all individuals, in the way of managing savings, mortgages or loans, and spending money in everyday life. The authorized sharing of customer data between the different actors has paved the way for the development of Fintech startups and other innovative players.

Looking at the regulatory framework, Open banking was initiated with the (Directive [EU] 2015/of the European Parliament and of the Council of November 25, 2015 on Payment Services in the Internal Market, Amending Directives 2002/65/EC, 2009/110/EC, and 2013/36/EU and Regulation [EU] No. 1093/2010, and Repealing Directive 2007/64/EC, n.d.), also known as Payment Services Directive 2 (PSD2), which entered into force since January 13, 2018 and has been fully operational since September 14, 2019.

The fundamental objectives of PSD2 were mainly to contribute to the dissemination of digital solutions and to instill confidence in the use of digital services; and facilitate and encourage competition in the finance industry by giving access to financial data, which were historically a prerogative of banks, even to third-party companies.

Since its implementation, banks are obliged to share information—provided customers' authorization—of their depositors with third parties (by the GDPR): banks are obliged to open their Application Programming Interface (API)[3] and customer data to these companies, thus

[3] Application Programming Interfaces (APIs) are a set of functions and procedures (essentially, a code string) that allow an application to access the functionality, data, and/or audience of other applications or digital services. An API that is accessible to anyone is called "open. "Nowadays when talking about APIs, we often refer to what are Open APIs, those APIs that make it possible for anyone to access the functionality or data of another company (e.g., Google makes the APIs available to integrate Google Maps-based maps into other sites).

reshaping the existing hierarchies in the relationship between consumers and financial institutions. It is from this crucial step that the idea of Open Banking draws its reason for being.

The services made accessible by the PDS2 Directive and, therefore, by the opening of APIs, are basically of three types:

- account information, to access bank accounts through applications other than banking;
- payment initiation, to place a payment order from the bank account through other applications;
- fund confirmation, to verify the presence of funds to cover the amount required for a transaction.

However, several banking players have already expanded their open APIs beyond the requirements of the PSD2, such as account-to-account money transfers, customer identification, instant insurance, and detailed business information.

Central to Open Banking are the providers of APIs, which are responsible for connecting companies not licensed with banking APIs through a "License as a service. "As expected, the startups and innovative companies operating in Fintech have taken on this role. There are, however, also actors traditionally "external" to the banking sector, such as large domestic sites and suppliers of gas and light. This demonstrates the concept of expanded competition behind Open Banking.

When the API provider is different from the one where the user holds his or her payment account or service—as in the case of Fintech—we talk about Third Party Provider (TTP). After collecting the user's consent, the TTP must have access to the payment account managed by an Account Servicing Payment Service Provider (ASPSP).

The service of providers is closely related to the type of Open Banking service, which is made mandatory by PSD2. It is possible to distinguish:

- PISPs (Payment Initiation Service Providers);
- AISPs (Account Information Service Providers);
- PIISPs (Payment Instrument Issuing Service Providers).

Several companies (not just startups) exploit this technology to be able to offer, for example, the ability to view all accounts (even on different banks) of a person in a single view. But the possibilities of Open Banking are numerous and apply to both consumers and financial traders.

3.2 *The Evolution of Open Banking: Toward Open Finance*

Open Finance is the open innovation applied to the whole financial and insurance sector (not only the banking one), which aims to capture all business opportunities arising from the use of resources (ideas, skills, data, etc.) external to the company. It is a holistic concept, starting from the idea of Open Banking, and evolving to embrace and include even less traditional actors. Not only banks and traditional players, but also startups, BigTech, car manufacturers, retailers, utilities, and anyone who proposes in the financial and insurance world, giving birth to an enlarged competition. This "journey" toward Open Finance is still "in progress" and, apparently, it will require a huge change of pace. PSD2 alone is not enough to produce the expected results. All the players involved must take, at least, these steps:

1. innovation must be a strategic process planned to make companies more competitive in the long term, including through strategic models that support innovation such as Design Thinking or the Blue Ocean Strategy, but not only;
2. innovation should not be limited to the bank account and payment banking services only, but applied to all financial services, starting with asset management or financial intermediation services, which are the most contiguous, but also the most "innovative" and not strictly banking like strong authentication, new insurance services, or all open commerce;
3. the innovation process must involve all actors around the financial world, not only startups but customers (corporate or consumer), universities, incubators, etc.

3.3 *The Academic Point of View on Open Banking*

The literature about Open Banking is the youngest among the studies regarding the spread of technologies in the financial industry, given the recent introduction of the PSD2 Directive by the European Regulator.

However, it is possible to mention some interesting papers that are trying to shed light on this "financial revolution."

Many studies about Open Banking so far have mainly focused on **technical implementation issues**, the rationale, and strategic implications from the regulators' and financial services providers' perspectives, whereas only a few of them have tried to investigate the consumers' intention to adopt Open Banking. According to (Borgogno & Colangelo, 2020), switching costs from incumbent traditional services to Open Banking services is one of the major reasons attributable to the inertia of banking consumers in the United Kingdom, although both the PSD2 Directive and the General Data Protection Regulation (GDPR) push for increased competition through a reduction of switching costs. Moreover, together with greater systems openness, Open Banking arrangements are also associated with unique vulnerabilities, such as greater exposure to new types of risks, like fraud, challenges in assigning liability when payments fail, and greater risk of consumer privacy loss due to the increased scope for a larger digital footprint that consumers leave behind due to expanded online interactions (Borgogno & Colangelo, 2020).

Looking at the **drivers of consumers' use** of Open Banking (Chan et al., 2022) develop a PLS-SEM model on 456 Australian survey respondents extending the Unified Theory of Acceptance and Use of Technology (Venkatesh et al., 2003) by integrating perceived risk, initial trust, and financial literacy into an overarching conceptual model. They find that performance expectancy (the degree to which individuals believe that using a system will help improve job performance), effort expectancy (the degree of ease associated with system use), social influence (the degree to which one perceives others believe they should use a new system), and perceived risk (the negative consequences that consumers perceive to be associated with situations of uncertainty) are direct antecedents of consumers' usage intention of Open Banking. Social influence has a strong mediating effect on usage intention through performance expectancy. The effect of perceived risk is alleviated by effort expectancy and initial trust (where trust is the extent to which one party is willing to depend on another with a feeling of relative security; [Jøsang & Presti, 2004]), while initial trust positively affects the effects of performance expectancy and effort expectancy on consumers' usage intention of Open Banking. Finally, financial literacy lowers initial trust toward Open Banking, possibly inducing consumer skepticism.

Continuing with **trust**, one of the principal implications of Open Banking is the enormous exposition of user information to all participating entities, a condition that requires investors' trust in the financial entities to be successful. According to (Kassab et al., 2022), there are 5 considerations that matter in affecting trust toward Open Ban. First, newcomers to this market space must receive a license from conduct authorities after demonstrating compliances with the data storage, business model, security, and IT practices policies, as well as possession of professional insurance. Since having this approval is not an easy task, once acquired, it can provide a signal that the TPP is to be trusted. Second, TPPs have some transparency obligations, regarding the type of information shared, with whom, and in what format, the possibility to adjust information sharing default settings, and what happens to the information after the customer decides to stop using the service or in case of an information breach. This type of transparency obligation enforces customers' trust. Third, trust may be negatively affected by the current disconnect between legal liability and practical rectification. For example, in cases when data have been transmitted by law by the financial intermediary to the TPP, the responsibility for data breaches by the TPP should not position the financial intermediary in liability. However, under the PSD2 Directive, regardless of whether an authorized transaction has occurred because of TPP access, the financial intermediary must still reimburse the customer, with the possibility to request compensation from TPP if it is found responsible. The burden of proof can rely upon the TPP to show that it was not responsible. Currently, an industry framework to administer such compensation claims has not yet emerged. Fourth, most investors are still not familiar with Open Banking, nor with its uses and benefits. Young customers seem more willing to use Open Banking services while older generations seem more reluctant. This generational aspect is another driver of trust. Finally, the trade-off between regulation and agility of the TPPs plays a role in instilling confidence in Open Banking: on one side, regulation can positively affect trust; on the other side, too much regulation can limit the TPPs' agility and their ability, above all the smaller ones, to be compliant with the regulatory requirements and survive in this new market space. The last—not less important—aspect is cybersecurity: since Open Banking implies access to all or most of an individual's financial assets, cybersecurity needs to be very strong to establish and maintain customers' trust.

4 Robo Advisory

4.1 A Definition of Robo-Advisory Services

This section explores another innovation in the financial services industry, i.e., robo advisory. Robo advisors can be generally defined as computer-automated investment platforms, where the typical user completes a questionnaire regarding his/her investment time horizon, goals, and risk tolerance, and then the robo advisor incorporates this information into a complex algorithm to generate an optimal customized investment solution. The main advantages of using these digital financial services have been acknowledged by the majority of investors in *higher cost-efficiency* and *easier accessibility*, two reasons that have forced traditional advisors to consider revising their fee structures and/or integrating robo-advisory platforms into their offerings to remain competitive in the market.

For many years, traditional advisors have based their services on developing deep relationships with clients over time, investing time in providing services and administrative and executive support, to consolidate trust with their clients and become irreplaceable. The client-advisor trust relationship has been studied extensively among academics and it has been proven to be determined by both economic and relational reasons (Cruciani et al., 2021): interestingly, some types of advisory (e.g., independent advisory) have shown to rely more on the relational drivers of trust and less on the economic and institutional ones. Despite this, some of the characteristics of the robo-advisory—easy accessibility, automated operations, and portfolio management, portfolio recommendations, low human involvement, and digitalized financial technology—seem to attract a large share of investors, thus contributing to the diversity of the financial services offered in the market (both planning and wealth management).

The diffusion of robo-advisory was also driven by other factors:

1. **The regulation**. Greater transparency for the customer, disclosure requirements, and limits to sales of complex products are creating new challenges and opportunities to force financial institutions to greater transparency and attention in determining their fees;
2. **Competition**. Interest rates at their minimum, the cost of funding, and the increasing cost of risk are making it more difficult for banks and financial institutions to generate profits. For this reason, they need to find new ways to generate positive returns for customers

and find low-cost investment strategies to manage those who are not served today;

3. **Technology**: the digital transformation is imposing an important review of the way of doing banking activity. In particular, the main technological changes are related to the use of social media and social networks, cloud computing, data analytics, and the omnichannel;
4. **Consumers' habits**. The average user has become more informed and careful. He/she uses all available means to retrieve and compare the information. Among users, millennials represent the category in which banks and financial institutions will have to look at in the medium term. They demand greater security, simplicity, customization, convenience, accessibility, and fewer constraints.

For all the above-mentioned reasons, the digitalization of the financial industry is growing very rapidly following patterns that differ on a geographical basis. If we look at the United States—the pioneers in the sector—it is possible to acknowledge a tendency to focus on portfolio management services targeted toward "disillusioned" investors, where the standard offering is characterized by a simplified direct-to-investment low-cost approach that allows clients to have an ETF portfolio in just a few clicks. The core clients are millennials, which are the most tech experts. Together with FinTechs, which seem to focus on developing automated asset allocation solutions, traditional players have digitized the advisory process allowing clients to have access to their investments and their financial advisors via remote solutions. Traditional players also offer more premium services such as the support of a human advisor and have higher entry requirements.

The situation is slightly different if we look at the Eurozone. In fact, the European market is highly fragmented with players offering both B2B and B2C services and with only two players (Nutmeg and Vaamo) offering services like those of their US counterparts. This fragmentation determined a no-set fee range, where most players differentiate among retail and institutional clients: low fees and low or no minimum initial investment requirement for the former and higher fees for the latter. In Europe, the use of financial communities, blogs, and other mediums of client engagement are common; the same is true for hybrid advisory models, where the traditional financial advisors still play an important role. Moreover, traditional banking services such as account aggregation are offered in more premium services.

4.2 *Business Models for Robo Advisory*

The more-than-10-year evolution of robo-advisory services gave rise to multiple business models that financial institutions can use to provide automated investment services. The differences may depend on several aspects, like the degree of independence, the inducement allowance, bank participation, human intervention, and the type of agreement applicable.

In particular:

1. **Independent robo advisors** are pure robo advisors, i.e., stand-alone legal entities with a high degree of independence. To benefit from this kind of service, the accounts are created in a bank chosen by the robo advisor or by the client. The robo-advisory firm oversees client profiling, portfolio construction, and periodic rebalancing. Clients must sign an investment advice and transmission of orders in an execution-only regime. As for the robo advisors' fees, they cannot receive inducements from the product manufacturer. All the policies such as privacy, suitability, systems, and risk control need to be defined by the robo advisor itself. Risk factors include structural costs, client acquisition costs, and greater compliance requirements. This model is suitable for the provision of portfolio management solutions (although formal authorization by the local regulator is required), the development of financial planning services (in particular the retirement ones), and the enhancement of wealth management services (including succession planning).
2. **Segregated robo advisors** are less independent with respect to independent robo advisors. In fact, the bank may hold distribution agreements with the product manufacturer. In the segregated model, there are two scenarios: (1) the bank does not retain inducements, and the robo advisor, which can be used as the bank's wealth management division, is independent—here the bank provides investment advice and transmission of orders in execution-only regime services by means of the robo advisor; (2) the bank keeps inducements and the robo advisor, being only a financial advisory division, is not independent. The bank provides investment advice and portfolio management by means of the robo advisor, while it keeps inducement being a distributor.
3. **Integrated robo advisors** are integrated into the bank's business model and represent only one of the online services the bank

provides. They do not exist outside the bank's service offering. The clients of the robo advisor are clients of the bank. The robo advisor can provide portfolio management, without any additional authorizations. The robo advisor can rely on bank procedures to regulate privacy policy and all the issues connected with monitoring and alerting systems. It is highly connected with the bank and its independence depends on bank decisions (e.g., if the bank wants to provide independent advice).

In addition to these types, there is a fourth one, where robo-advisory platforms are used only as a tool:

4. **The Robo 4 Advice**. The platform is used just as a support by a human advisor who provides recommendations. The advice is not fully automated, since the provider of advice is the consultant, not the platform. However, the platform can be used by the final customer as a digital channel to the bank. Independency concerns the human advisor status, not the platform's one. The robo advisor is only a portfolio manager. The suggested portfolio can be accepted or not. Portfolio management can be facilitated by the robo advisor, and it depends on the restrictions of the platform. The suitability of the advice is ensured by the consultant. There is no obligatory connection between the robo advisor and a bank. The advice agreement is between the consultant and the client. Commission fees are paid to the consultant for the advice.

4.3 The Academic Point of View on Robo Advisory

The research on robo advisory has grown significantly in the last few years. Academics have reflected on different aspects of this type of service.

Looking at the studies that investigate **users' demographics**, it is not unanimously accepted that robo-advisory users are significantly different from traditional advisory users. According to (D'Acunto et al., 2019), they are similar in terms of overall demographics, whereas other studies prove exactly the opposite. In particular, the moderating dimensions of robo-advisory usage are age, general education, financial expertise, confidence, **risktolerance**, income, and current capital/portfolio values. Concerning age, studies show that the typical users of robo-advisory services are young people (Brenner & Meyll, 2020; Fulk et al., 2018), while (Fan & Chatterjee, 2020) describe young users as aged "under

65." As far as education is concerned, higher education seems to positively influence the probability to use robo advisory (Lourenço et al., 2020), together with higher (self-perceived) financial education or financial literacy (Fan & Chatterjee, 2020; Lourenço et al., 2020). However, other studies are skeptical about the effect of robo advisory on investors' competencies, claiming that this type of advisory makes them passive and less financially literate and educated (Tan, 2020). (D'Hondt et al., 2020) show that individuals with low education and low income are those that benefit the most by using robo advisors. Also, personal characteristics like having high confidence (i.e., being less financially impulsive and more strategic with financial decision-making) seem to positively affect the use of automated advisory (Fulk et al., 2018; Woodyard & Grable, 2018). Focusing on risk tolerance (Fan & Chatterjee, 2020) show that individuals with higher risk tolerance are more likely to use a robo-advisory service. Finally (Brenner & Meyll, 2020; Fulk et al., 2018) show that those with lower income and lower capital and portfolio values are more likely to adopt robo-advisory services. Interestingly, if individuals hold inherited money, they are more likely to rely on traditional advisors (Fulk et al., 2018) as the unexpected capital increase is not paired with an appropriate increase in financial education or confidence in financial decision-making. Finally (Waliszewski & Warchlewska, 2020) analyze socio-economic factors and find that nationality affects the likelihood to rely on robo advisors: countries with a higher level of acceptance for robo-advice include Turkey, the Czech Republic, Romania, and the United States. The remaining countries have a lower acceptance rate, with Austria and Luxembourg having the lowest. Moreover, gender is related to the likelihood to use robo-advisory services, with men being more likely than women. Finally, more people in a household translate into a greater probability to use robo advisory.

Despite the interesting findings just presented, some authors find that the share of robo-advisory users compared to investors seeking traditional financial advice is typically very small. (Woodyard & Grable, 2018), for example, find that only 5% of a US financial capability study were users of robo advisory, while the remaining participants were users of traditional in-person financial advice. Similar results are found by (Waliszewski & Warchlewska, 2020) and by (Niszczota & Kaszás, 2020), who claim that the financial sector suffers from an algorithm aversion, determining a barrier to adopting innovative FinTech solutions. On the contrary (Brenner & Meyll, 2020), using representative investor data, investigate if robo advisors might be a substitute for traditional in-person financial advisory and find that robo advisors represent a valid alternative for seeking investment advice, especially among those investors who are worried about the conflicts of interest present in the traditional advice.

Another stream of literature in robo advisory focuses on the factors that influence **users' adoption and acceptance**, identifying the level of trust, transparency, ease of use, usefulness, and robo advisor's expertise to be the most significant. Trust is one of the most investigated factors and the main contributions distinguish between trust in technologies or trust in the robo-advisory provider that together moderate trust in robo advisory, enhancing the adoption and acceptance of automated or semi-automated advisory (Guo et al., 2019). The literature has also investigated if the humanization of robo advisors (attributing an avatar and a name, for example) affects trust. Some studies do not find significant positive effects of humanizing the robo advisor, others instead do, especially if the task that the advisor must perform has a low complexity (Hodge et al., 2021). (Morana et al., 2020) find a similar result: higher humanization increases the perceived social presence and trusting beliefs. Moreover, trusting beliefs impact significantly the acceptance of the robo advisor's recommendation. Also, the communication style of the robo advisor seems to play a role on trust: the usage of conversational robo advisors, where the communication style is more like the human one, positively affects trust, thus enhancing robo-advisory adoption and recommendation acceptance (Hildebrand & Bergner, 2021). Another critical issue is transparency: in fact, when robo advisors provide more information on how they work and financial education as well, potential users are more willing to use this kind of services (Litterscheidt & Streich, 2020). Moreover, when the understanding of robo-advisory processes and familiarity with AI-based systems is high, it is more likely that individuals perceive its usage as easy, influencing its perceived usefulness. Both factors have a positive effect on the attitude toward robo advisors, which significantly enhances the intention to use them (Belanche et al., 2019). Finally, psychological factors like positive and negative emotions (e.g., respectively, joy or anxiety) in expected use, respectively, increase/decrease the adoption of robo-advisory services (Hohenberger et al., 2019).

After looking at the demographic factors and at the determinants of trust in robo advisors' advice, another stream of research looks at the *service characteristics*, distinguishing between the different phases of the process design. Starting from *initiationand profiling*, some authors show that, because of the absence of human interaction and the importance of trust in financial advisory, providers of robo-advisory services improve the initiation process by giving information about the whole advisory process, products used, and costs associated with the services, enhancing its transparency (Jung et al., 2018; Litterscheidt & Streich, 2020). (Belanche et al., 2019) also indicate that robo advisors should consider the user's familiarity with AI-based systems and provide ad-hoc support, e.g., by employing chatbots (Morana et al., 2020). Concerning risk profiling, many authors have strongly criticized the reliability of robo advisors' profiling techniques. According to (Beketov et al., 2018), robo advisors often use simple static online questionnaires to define an investors' risk profile, something that is questioned by several authors, who claim that this way of profiling investors alone is not sufficient. Other authors suggest hybrid approaches, where human communication is used to enhance the conversion rate of robo advisors (Beketov et al., 2018; Jung et al., 2018) or metaphors and scenario-based questions with visualizations. This evidence shows that robo advisors tend to balance between the simplicity and sophistication of the questionnaires (D'Acunto et al., 2019). Tertilt and Scholz (2018) investigate the questions asked by robo advisors and claim that they are differentiated between general information, risk capacity, and risk tolerance of the investor. They also assess the correlation between questions and risk assessment and find that only approximately 60% of questions impact the risk assessment, thus showing that a better individualization of profiling would be recommended.

Other studies look at the *matching and customization* of the service, a step of the advice process that many consider a "black box" (D'Acunto et al., 2019; Jung et al., 2018). Some authors claim that, for the sake of transparency, these algorithms should be open (Litterscheidt & Streich, 2020). Other authors criticize the quality of the service: (Beketov et al., 2018), for example, show that over 80% of robo advisors base their recommendation on typical portfolio allocation methods (like Modern Portfolio Theory), although more sophisticated portfolio allocation methods attract more affluent users.

Finally, the studies about the *monitoring and rebalancing* phase show that, on one side, being the monitoring delegated to an algorithm, the consequences of behavioral biases and irrational human behavior should be reduced. Normally, the robo advisor rebalances the portfolios at fixed time intervals, e.g., quarterly or yearly, and after trigger events, e.g., market or user changes. Concerning the quality of the service, the evidence is mixed: (D'Acunto et al., 2019) found that portfolios managed by a robo advisor are more diversified and perform better compared to self-monitored portfolios of individual investors (D'Acunto et al., 2019; Reher et al., 2018). Instead (Puhle, 2019) found that portfolio allocations with similar risk preferences vary greatly between robo advisors, but that no robo advisors could beat their benchmark index between 2015 and 2018, even before considering fees. Interestingly, (D'Hondt et al., 2020) simulated robo advisors' investment decision-making, and found that the 2008 financial crisis would have been surpassed by robo advisors with fewer losses than their employed passive index strategy.

There are also studies that concentrate on the *overall robo-advisory design*, which means the criteria that are overarching the robo-advisory process phases. These criteria include the robo-advisory design decisions concerning the degree of delegation and automation, the degree of humanization, including conversational abilities and designs to mitigate behavioral biases. For an extensive review of this issue, see (Rühr et al., 2019). Interestingly, they show that processes requiring constant attention and immediate action, such as rebalancing, tend to be highly automated and delegated. In contrast, profiling tends to be only partially delegated, often supported by humans, to mitigate potential errors. Moreover, robo advisors are often designed with a certain degree of humanization, which was found to impact robo-advisory adoption and recommendation acceptance. For example, (Hodge et al., 2021) prove that even a low degree of humanization, e.g., naming the RA, could increase its adoption. Research also investigated robo-advisory designs with more human characteristics employed (e.g., showing an avatar or providing chatbot functionality with social cues, like having a dynamic response time) and found that recommendation acceptance and invested capital amount increase (Morana et al., 2020). For even higher degrees of humanization, robo advisors need to understand and process speech, imitating face-to-face conversations in traditional financial advice, to improve customer-advisor interactions. (Hildebrand & Bergner, 2021) show that in the evaluation of their conversational robo-advisory design, the users perceived the robo advisor and its provider as more trustworthy, recording greater recommendation acceptance as well as an increase in invested capital in comparison to a non-conversational robo advisor. Design also affects the way in which robo advisors tend to reduce behavioral biases of its users and can implement nudges, i.e., default values and warning messages to reduce, for example, decision inertia, which is the unwillingness to use new information in decision-making. Moreover, some studies show that portfolios managed by robo advisors decrease the tendency to sell extreme winning and losing positions (the rank effect), the disposition effect (tendency to realize gains more often than losses), and to a small degree trend chasing (the tendency to buy position after its price increases) (D'Acunto et al., 2019). The robo advisor might also control the "Performance-Control Dilemma," by maximizing the user perception of control while limiting its actual deviation possibilities from recommendations, for example, with personalized anchors. This is particularly interesting for investors with low financial literacy, who most of the times are also risk averse and low-budget users, for whom the robo advisors need to be designed in an easy-to-use and understandable way, providing financial advice efficiently and transparently.

While discussing about the service, it is also worth mentioning the role played by the *provider* and its most important specific characteristics. First of all, robo advisors are distributed by different firm types, for example, FinTech startups, established investment companies (e.g., "Vanguard" and "BlackRock"), or incumbent banks (Guo et al., 2019). The adoption of and satisfaction with robo advisors rely significantly on its provider's trust, moderated by its reputation, integrity, and firm type. For example, (Guo et al., 2019) found a higher effect of expertise for established financial companies in contrast to startups. Instead, (Lourenço et al., 2020) also distinguished between firm types and found that profit-oriented firms need to provide more arguments for trust-building and expertise than non-profit-oriented firms and product-provider firms are considered more trustworthy and competent than advisor-only firms.

As we saw speaking about Fintech, the business model of the robo-advisory provider can be divided into B2C or B2B. While B2C providers deliver their services directly to end-customers, B2B robo-advisory providers develop "white label" Information Services (IS), that can be used, e.g., by traditional financial advisors or banks to provide robo-advisory services (Phoon & Koh, 2018). Since financial market regulations are different across the world, the robo advisor providers distribute their robo services separately for each national market. In contrast to traditional advice, robo advisors generate value because of the widening of the client base giving basic financial advice at affordable prices. Moreover, in contrast with traditional financial advice that tends to have very high minimum investment amounts, robo-advisory providers lower this minimum required capital amount. As an example,

(Reher et al., 2018) found that a reduction in minimum account size of 90% led to a substantial increase in new account creations while also increasing the total deposit flow, despite the reduction of per-portfolio balances.

The last stream of research looks at *competition* and at the reactions of traditional advisors to the robo-advisory phenomenon. First, it is interesting to note that many authors find changes in the education and training of human financial advisors, assisting to the use of Robo for Advisory, i.e., robo-advisory technologies as decision support tools for the human advisors (Britton & Atkinson, 2017). These findings seem to support the idea of the "hybrid model", i.e., a model that balances human and algorithmic components, suggesting that full automation may not be the preferred option because of its creative and social limits (see, e.g., [Coombs & Redman, 2018]). Consequently, robo advisors seem to augment rather than substitute human financial advisors. Moreover, several studies investigate the various advantages and disadvantages of robo advisory and find that, among advantages, it is possible to acknowledge the possibility of making passive investments at low consulting costs and low minimum investment amounts (Waliszewski & Warchlewska, 2020). Second, robo advisors deliver less emotional decision-making and convenient service with instant satisfaction of informational needs. As previously mentioned, (Niszczota & Kaszás, 2020) find a general aversion against robo advisory, especially when moral recommendations are sought, e.g., in the case of ESG portfolio allocations. This is opposite to the findings of (Waliszewski & Warchlewska, 2020) who show that users of robo advisory perceive robo advisors as more ethical or at least equally ethical compared to human advisors.

In contrast to traditional financial advice, two big limits of robo-advisory services are to be acknowledged in the limited range of financial planning services and lack of the full adjustment to the user's individual needs. Robo advisors are less accurate in making quality questions than its traditional human competition, which leads to less customized and sophisticated financial advice or even failing fulfilling its fiduciary duties.

5 The Regulatory Framework

5.1 *The Payment Services Directive (PSD2)*

As described in the previous sections, the financial services industry is undergoing a massive revolution that was triggered by the PSD2 Directive.

The PSD2 (Payment Services Directive) is the second Payment Services Directive, which came into force in the European Union on January 13, 2016, with a deadline for transposition in the Member States two years later. It is part of the modernization of the legislative framework of the European retail payments market, aimed at developing secure, efficient, competitive, and innovative electronic payment systems for consumers, businesses, and merchants.

The areas of major novelty of PSD2 compared to the first Payment Services Directive (PSD1) are related to the new security procedures for access to the online account and electronic payments and the new payment services offered in the area of e-commerce and online shopping from banks and new market players.

The PSD2 leaves to the European Banking Authority (EBA) the definition of a wide corpus of secondary legislation (Regulatory Technical Standards—RTS, Implementing Technical Standards—ITS, Guidelines), among which the (*Commission Delegated Regulation (EU) 2018/389—of November 27, 2017—Supplementing Directive (EU) 2015/2366 of the European Parliament and of the Council with regard to Regulatory Technical Standards for Strong Customer Authentication and Common and Secure Open Standards of Communication*, n.d.), published in the Official Journal of the European Union on March 13, 2018, which integrates the PSD2 with reference to regulatory technical standards on Strong Customer Authentication (SCA) and open standards of common and secure communication (Common Secure Communication—CSC) between Account Servicing Payment Service Providers (ASPSP) and Payment Initiation Service Providers (PISP), Account Information Service Providers (AISP) and Card Issuer Service Providers (CISP).

The Regulation entered into force on March 14, 2018 and was implemented on September 14, 2019. It specifies and details:

- the requirements for strong customer authentication;

- exemptions from the application of strong authentication based on the level of service-related risk, the amount and/or frequency of the transaction, and the payment channel;
- the confidentiality and integrity requirements of custom security credentials;
- the requirements for common and secure open standards of communication for the purposes of identification, authentication, notification, and transmission of information, as well as for the implementation of security measures, between the different payment service providers involved (i.e., ASPSP, PISP, AISP, CISP).

The first innovation is the offer of new payment services, regulated by PSD2:

- payment initiation services (Payment Initiation Services—PIS) that enable an online payment to be initiated via a payment service provider other than the one with which the account is held,
- information services on online payment accounts (Account Information Services—AIS) on the basis of which aggregate information can be obtained on one or more online accounts held also at different institutions,
- availability confirmation services funds provided in the case of payments made with debit cards issued by a different operator than the one with which the account is held (i.e., the CISP).

New regulated traders—PISP/AISP/CISP—then provide services on portions of the payment chain, accessing information about customers' online accounts. Account Servicing Payment Service Providers must make this information accessible through dedicated interfaces (c.d. Application Programming Interface—API) or via the user interface in use, amended according to the new rules.

The second change concerns the strengthening of security measures in online payment services. To make online transactions more secure, increase customer confidence and thus stimulate their use, also considering the introduction of new services and new subjects, more security safeguards appeared to be necessary. As a result, new customer authentication (SCA) and online payment authorization methods have been introduced since September 14, 2019.

In practice, PSD2 introduces an obligation for banks and other payment service providers to implement two or more different-factor authentication systems. Username and password alone are no longer sufficient to access online accounts or to make a payment and must therefore be accompanied by at least an additional authentication element of different type, such as the fingerprint or the use of a personal device such as the smartphone. In addition, for distance transactions an additional unique code is added that dynamically connects the amount and payee. The challenge for operators is to provide digital payments with this level of security without compromising user friendliness.

5.2 The Revised Guidelines on Suitability by ESMA (2018)

If on one side the PDS2 increased competition and the sharing of customers' data, on the other side the need to guarantee investor protection and the suitability of the products and services offered could not be neglected. Looking at robo advisory—i.e., the provision of investment advice or portfolio management services (in whole or in part) through an automated or semi-automated system used as a client-facing tool—the main efforts of the Regulator have been exactly in this direction. In fact, the assessment of **suitability** was already a crucial exercise under MiFID I and II. However, in May 2018, right after the adoption of MiFID II, ESMA published a revised version of the guidelines, broadening the 2012 guidelines in order to consider the technological developments of the advisory market driven by the increasing use of automated or semi-automated systems for the provision of investment advice or portfolio management (robo-advice). The aim of the revised guidelines was "to ensure a common, uniform and consistent implementation of the MiFID II requirements related to the assessment of suitability by providing explanations, clarifications and examples on how the relevant obligations related to the assessment of suitability should be fulfilled" (ESMA 35-43-869, p. 7). By doing this, ESMA aimed at enforcing the correct implementation by companies of these requirements. The guidelines also aimed to achieve a convergent approach in the supervision of the suitability requirements by competent authorities, as greater convergence may lead to improved investor protection (consumer outcomes).

In the Supporting Guidelines to General Guideline 1, paragraphs 20–22 (ibid, pp. 37–38), ESMA has clearly stated that to address potential gaps in clients' understanding of the services provided through robo-advice, firms should inform them of the following specific aspects:

a. a very clear explanation of the exact degree and extent of human involvement and if and how the client can ask for human interaction;
b. an explanation that the answers clients provide will have a direct impact in determining the suitability of the investment decisions recommended or undertaken on their behalf;
c. a description of the sources of information used to generate an investment advice or to provide the portfolio management service (e.g., if an online questionnaire is used, firms should explain that the responses to the questionnaire may be the sole basis for the robo-advice or whether the firm has access to other client information or accounts);
d. an explanation of how and when the client's information will be updated with regard to his situation, personal circumstances, etc.

Moreover, firms providing robo-advice should pay particular attention to the effectiveness of their disclosure policies in particular by: emphasizing the relevant information (e.g., through the use of design features such as popup boxes); considering whether some information should be accompanied by interactive text (e.g., through the use of design features such as tooltips), or other means to provide additional details to clients who are seeking further information (e.g., through F.A.Q. section).

Finally, robo-advisory firms are expected to properly design their questionnaires, to be able to gather the necessary information to know their clients. This may imply for them to consider whether the information collected through the online questionnaire allows the firm to conclude that the advice provided is suitable for their clients based on their knowledge and experience, their financial situation, and their investment objectives and needs. Secondly, whether the questions in the questionnaire are sufficiently clear and/or whether the questionnaire is designed to provide additional clarification or examples to clients when necessary (e.g., using of design features, such as tooltips or popup boxes). Thirdly, whether some human interaction (including remote interaction via emails or mobile phones) is available to clients when responding to the online questionnaire. Lastly, whether steps have been taken to address inconsistent client responses (such as incorporating in the questionnaire design features to alert clients when their responses appear internally inconsistent and suggest them to reconsider such responses; or implementing systems to automatically flag apparently inconsistent information provided by a client for review or follow-up by the firm).

Another relevant aspect that must be treated with caution by robo advisors is the client's tendency to overestimate their knowledge and experience, a risk that is expected to be higher when clients provide information through an automated (or semi-automated) system, especially in situations where very limited or no human interaction at all between clients and the firm's employees is foreseen. This implies a bigger effort by robo advisors in designing proper questionnaires, aimed at effectively assessing clients' understanding of the risks and characteristics of the financial products and services.

Some of these requirements seemed to concern the main players in the market: in fact, some of them, who participated in the consultation that preceded the release of the new guidelines, pointed out the risk of information overload and that the adoption by firms of a prescriptive approach could represent a risk that "might result in clients being provided with long and unengaging documents that are neither useful nor user-friendly" (ibid, p. 13). Several respondents observed that the average retail investor would not be in the position to fully understand and evaluate the characteristics and the efficiency of algorithms used by robo advisors, and therefore not all information should be provided. However, ESMA replied that the provision of information to clients is important to enable them to make informed investment decisions. The way to reduce information overload is to allow for some information to be provided in a standardized format, for example at the beginning of the contractual relationship. ESMA also confirms that it is not its intention to require firms to disclose their algorithms in detail to clients.

Another important topic in the revised guidelines regards the framework of regulation and supervision to be used: according to some automated players in the market that responded to the consultation, robo advisors should share the same framework as traditional advisors, especially on the topic of suitability. They believe that the additional guidance required by the guidelines may result in an additional burden without offering higher protection. Some other respondents, instead, considered that Supporting Guidelines to General Guideline 1, paragraphs 20–22 should be related to robo-advice only.

6 Conclusions

This chapter has drawn a complete picture of how Fintech, Open Banking/Finance, and robo advisory are challenging the traditional banking services. On one side, the European Regulator is fueling increased competition in the market—and the PSD2 Directive (2016) was a clear proof of that. On the other side, automated financial services and Open Banking are imposing further "threats" on investors, like, for example, the protection of their data, the correct risk profiling when they use robo-advisory services, the trust in the algorithms that match their risk profile with an investment recommendation, etc. In this regard, the Regulator has revised the Guidelines on Suitability in 2018 to consider these new players, thus guaranteeing investors' protection and the correct functioning of the market. However, it is still not clear how much technologies will disrupt the traditional banking system and the financial services industry. The academic debate acknowledges the numerous advantages of Fintech, Open Banking, and robo advisory but still seems to believe that traditional banks and in-person advisors are not at risk: automated services cannot substitute traditional services, rather a "hybrid model" is what seems to best meet the needs of all types of customers.

References

Basel Committee on Banking Supervision. (2018). *Sound practices implications of fintech developments for banks and bank supervisors*. www.bis.org

Beketov, M., Lehmann, K., & Wittke, M. (2018). Robo advisors: Quantitative methods inside the robots. *Journal of Asset Management, 19*(6), 363–370. https://doi.org/10.1057/s41260-018-0092-9

Belanche, D., Casaló, L., & Flavián, C. (2019). Artificial Intelligence in FinTech: Understanding robo-advisors adoption among customers. *Industrial Management and Data Systems, 119*(7), 1411–1430. https://doi.org/10.1108/IMDS-08-2018-0368

Borgogno, O., & Colangelo, G. (2020). *Consumer inertia and competition-sensitive data governance: The case of open banking*. www.accc.gov.au/focus-areas/inquiries-ongoing/digital-platforms-in

Brenner, L., & Meyll, T. (2020). Robo-advisors: A substitute for human financial advice? *Journal of Behavioral and Experimental Finance, 25*, 100275. https://doi.org/10.1016/j.jbef.2020.100275

Britton, B. L., & Atkinson, D. G. (2017). An investigation into the significant impacts of automation in asset management. *Journal of Economic and Social Development, 4*(1), 2–14. http://www.jesd-online.com

Chan, R., Troshani, I., Rao Hill, S., & Hoffmann, A. (2022). Towards an understanding of consumers' FinTech adoption: The case of open banking. *International Journal of Bank Marketing, 40*(4), 886–917. https://doi.org/10.1108/IJBM-08-2021-0397

Coombs, C., & Redman, A. (2018). *The impact of robo-advice on financial advisers: A qualitative case study*. https://aisel.aisnet.org/ukais2018/17

D'Acunto, F., Prabhala, N., & Rossi, A. G. (2019). The promises and Pitfalls of robo-advising. In *Review of financial studies* (Vol. 32, Issue 5, pp. 1983–2020). Oxford University Press. https://doi.org/10.1093/rfs/hhz014

D'Hondt, C., de Winne, R., Ghysels, E., & Raymond, S. (2020). Artificial intelligence alter egos: Who might benefit from robo-investing? *Journal of Empirical Finance, 59*, 278–299. https://doi.org/10.1016/j.jempfin.2020.10.002

Dapp, T. F., Slomka, L., & Hoffmann, R. (2014). Current issues digital economy and structural change. *Deutsche Bank Research, 11*, 1–39. http://www.bmbf.de/de/23173.php

Fan, L., & Chatterjee, S. (2020). The utilization of robo-advisors by individual investors: An analysis using diffusion of innovation and information search frameworks. *Journal of Financial Counseling and Planning, 31*(1), 130–145. https://doi.org/10.1891/JFCP-18-00078

Fulk, M., Grable, J. E., Watkins, K., & Kruger, M. (2018). Financial services review who uses robo-advisory services, and who does not? *Financial Services Review, 27*, 173–188.

Guo, F., Cheng, X., & Zhang, Y. (2019). *A conceptual model of trust influencing factors in robo-advisor products: A qualitative study*. https://aisel.aisnet.org/whiceb2019

Gupta, R., Mejia, C., Gianchandani, Y. B., & Kajikawa, Y. (2021). Ambidextrous firm strategy insights from internet of things linked interfirm deals. *IEEE Transactions on Engineering Management*. https://doi.org/10.1109/TEM.2020.3041250

Hildebrand, C., & Bergner, A. (2021). Conversational robo advisors as surrogates of trust: Onboarding experience, firm perception, and consumer financial decision making. *Journal of the Academy of Marketing Science, 49*, 659–676. https://doi.org/10.1007/s11747-020

Hodge, F. D., Mendoza, K. I., & Sinha, R. K. (2021). The effect of humanizing robo-advisors on investor judgments. *Contemporary Accounting Research, 38*(1), 770–792. https://doi.org/10.1111/1911-3846.12641

Hohenberger, C., Lee, C., & Coughlin, J. F. (2019). Acceptance of robo-advisors: Effects of financial experience, affective reactions, and self-enhancement motives. *Financial Planning Review, 2*(2). https://doi.org/10.1002/cfp2.1047

Jack, W., & Suri, T. (2014). Risk sharing and transactions costs: Evidence from Kenya's mobile money revolution. *American Economic Review, 104*(1), 183–223. https://doi.org/10.1257/aer.104.1.183

Jøsang, A., & Presti, S. l. (2004). *Analysing the relationship between risk and trust*. https://doi.org/10.1007/978-3-540-24747-0_11

Jung, D., Dorner, V., Weinhardt, C., & Pusmaz, H. (2018). Designing a robo-advisor for risk-averse, low-budget consumers. *Electronic Markets, 28*(3), 367–380. https://doi.org/10.1007/s12525-017-0279-9

Kassab, M., Laplante, P., & Voas, J. (2022). Trust considerations in open banking. *IT Professional, 24*(1), 70–73. https://doi.org/10.1109/MITP.2021.3136015

Lee, I., & Shin, Y. J. (2018). Fintech: Ecosystem, business models, investment decisions, and challenges. *Business Horizons, 61*(1), 35–46. https://doi.org/10.1016/j.bushor.2017.09.003

Legner, C., Eymann, T., Hess, T., Matt, C., Böhmann, T., Drews, P., Mädche, A., Urbach, N., & Ahlemann, F. (2017). Digitalization: Opportunity and challenge for the business and information systems engineering community. *Business and Information Systems Engineering, 59*(4), 301–308. https://doi.org/10.1007/s12599-017-0484-2

Liberti, J. M., & Petersen, M. A. (2019). Information: Hard and soft. *Review of Corporate Finance Studies, 8*(1), 1–41. https://doi.org/10.1093/rcfs/cfy009

Litterscheidt, R., & Streich, D. J. (2020). Financial education and digital asset management: What's in the black box? *Journal of Behavioral and Experimental Economics, 87*, 101573. https://doi.org/10.1016/j.socec.2020.101573

Lourenço, C. J. S., Dellaert, B. G. C., & Donkers, B. (2020). Whose algorithm says so: The relationships between type of firm, perceptions of trust and expertise, and the acceptance of financial robo-advice. *Journal of Interactive Marketing, 49*, 107–124. https://doi.org/10.1016/j.intmar.2019.10.003

Morana, S., Gnewuch, U., & Jung, D. (2020). *The effect of anthropomorphism on investment decision-making with robo-advisor chatbots designing conversational dashboards to support effective use view project designing user assistance view project*. https://www.researchgate.net/publication/341277570

Murinde, V., Rizopoulos, E., & Zachariadis, M. (2022). The impact of the FinTech revolution on the future of banking: Opportunities and risks. *International Review of Financial Analysis, 81*, 102103. https://doi.org/10.1016/j.irfa.2022.102103

Navaretti, G. B., Calzolari, G., Mansilla-Fernández, J. M., & Pozzolo, A. F. (2018). *FinTech and banking. Friends or foes?* SSRN.

Niszczota, P., & Kaszás, D. (2020). Robo-investment aversion. *PLoS ONE, 15*(9 September). https://doi.org/10.1371/journal.pone.0239277

Phoon, K., & Koh, F. (2018). Robo-advisors and wealth management. *Journal of Alternative Investments, 20*(3), 79–94. https://doi.org/10.3905/jati.201

Puhle, M. (2019). The performance and asset allocation of German robo-advisors. *Society and Economy, 41*(3), 331–351. https://doi.org/10.1556/204.2019.41.3.4

Puri, M., & Rocholl, J. (2008). On the importance of retail banking relationships. *Journal of Financial Economics, 89*(2), 253–267. https://doi.org/10.1016/j.jfineco.2007.07.005

Reher, M., Sun, C., Campbell, J., Friedman, B., Gete, P., Gilchrist, D., Jurek, J., Shleifer, A.-D., Sokolinski, S., Stein, J., & Vallee, B. (2018). *Automated financial management: diversification and account size flexibility.* https://ssrn.com/abstract=2872134

Roengpitya, R., Tarashev, N., Tsatsaronis, K., & Villegas, A. (2017). *Bank business models: popularity and performance.* www.bis.org

Rühr, A., Streich, D., Berger, B., & Hess, T. (2019). *A classification of decision automation and delegation in digital investment management systems.* https://hdl.handle.net/10125/59584

Shin, H. S. (2019). *Big tech in finance: Opportunities and risks.* BIS.

Suri, T., & Jack, W. (2016). *The long-run poverty and gender impacts of mobile money.* https://www.science.org

Tan, G. K. S. (2020). Robo-advisors and the financialization of lay investors. *Geoforum, 117*, 46–60. https://doi.org/10.1016/j.geoforum.2020.09.004

Thakor, A. V. (2020). Fintech and banking: What do we know? *Journal of Financial Intermediation, 41*, 100833. https://doi.org/10.1016/j.jfi.2019.100833

Thaler, R. H., & Sunstein, C. R. (2003). Libertarian paternalism. *American Economic Review, 93*, 2.

Tilson, D., Lyytinen, K., & Sørensen, C. (2010). Digital infrastructures: The missing IS research agenda. *Information Systems Research, 21*(4), 748–759. https://doi.org/10.1287/isre.1100.0318

Venkatesh, V. H., Morris, M. G., Davis, G. B., & Davis, F. D. (2003). USER acceptance of information technology: Toward a unified view. *MIS Quarterly, 27*(3), 425–478.

Waliszewski, K., & Warchlewska, A. (2020). Attitudes towards artificial intelligence in the area of personal financial planning: A case study of selected countries. *Entrepreneurship and Sustainability Issues, 8*(2), 399–420. https://doi.org/10.9770/jesi.2020.8.2(24)

Woodyard, A. S., & Grable, J. E. (2018). Insights into the users of robo-advisory firms. *Journal of Financial Service Professionals, 72*(5), 56–66.

World Economic Forum. (2015). *The future of financial services. How disruptive innovations are reshaping the way financial services are structured, provisioned and consumed*. www.deloitte.com/about

Wray, P., Director, M., Budesha, L., Thomas, A., Analyst, L., Yu, Y., Lebefromm, R., Loh, I., Analyst, J. H., de Stefano, G., & Bravo, C. (2021). *Fintech control tower (FCT) BCG Q3 2021*. Fintech.

CHAPTER 5

Challenges and Opportunities for the Future Investor: A Practitioner's Guide

Abstract This chapter presents the results of a questionnaire launched in June 2022 targeted to European financial professionals. The questionnaire includes two sections dealing with specific questions regarding the challenges and opportunities of sustainable finance and financial digitalization, with a deeper focus on robo advisory and Open Finance. The questions have been devised focusing on the themes emerged in the reviews of the regulatory developments and academic research conducted in Chapters 3 and 4 to explore practitioners' views on these important topics. Given the relevance of stakeholders' feedback in the finetuning of the regulatory activities within the European Union, the survey offers the opportunity to feel the temperature of the practitioners' views before several of the new regulatory requirements become mandatory.

Keywords Survey · Sustainable finance · Robo advisory · Practitioners

© The Author(s), under exclusive license to Springer Nature Switzerland AG 2022

C. Cruciani et al., *Understanding Financial Risk Tolerance*,
https://doi.org/10.1007/978-3-031-13131-8_5

1 The Survey

1.1 Some Reasons Why

This book sets out to explore the drivers behind the evolution of risk tolerance measures within the domain of financial advisory: after reviewing the regulatory changes and describing how much (or little) academic research had contributed to them, we entered the realm of speculation and identified two themes that are currently very likely to affect the way in which financial advice is provided—sustainable finance and fintech.

Reviewing the current legislative developments and highlighting the timeline for the application of the new rules is useful in describing the pressure financial advisors must face in terms of compliance but does not yet shed sufficient light on how some of these changes are going to be implemented in practice and which practical hurdles financial advisors will have to face. Moreover, the European legislation and academia seem to have reduced their distance in the relative visions they hold about measuring financial risk tolerance. Thus, a question arises: are these new challenges likely to be neutral for the evaluation of clients' risk tolerance and more importantly for their engagement with this new vision of European finance? We provided some partial answers at the end of the previous two chapters regarding sustainable finance and robo advisory, but this chapter will try to provide a more holistic view on the matter discussing the last piece of the puzzle—what do advisors think? How are they facing these new challenges?

Stakeholders' engagement has always been key in deploying the full potential of European law and regulations and we believe that this chapter presents a useful contribution to this ongoing debate.

1.2 Survey Structure and Participant Pool

1.2.1 General Information

The survey was available in three languages (English, Italian, and French) through the Qualtrics platform in June 2022. It was launched after a short event discussing the key relevant themes for financial advisory in Italy organized with Wieldmore Investment Management on LinkedIn but was later sent out to several other financial professionals located in Europe. Filling out the survey was voluntary and was not incentivized in any way other than allowing for participation in a second webinar discussing the key themes that emerged.

The survey includes two content sections and one socio-demographic section. The first section includes 5 questions regarding sustainable finance, the second section includes 3 questions on robo advisory and 2 questions on open finance and the socio-demographic question. The types of questions included range from multiple-choice questions to Likert scale and open-ended questions. All questions are framed within regulatory changes, with general details provided; only one question includes a hypothetical scenario regarding Open Finance, which, as Chapter 4 discussed, is currently not clearly defined. All answers were required to move on to the following question, each question was presented in a different page, and it was not possible to go back to previous questions once the answer was provided. The complete list of questions is available as an Appendix to this chapter.

1.2.2 The Sustainable-Finance Section

The section on sustainable finance dealt with some perceptions regarding the investor features that make individuals more well suited for this type of investment. Question 1 asked to express the level of agreement with four different statements: the first three regard the existence of specific levels of risk tolerance, time horizon, and tolerance to losses that make a client not suited for sustainable investment. The fourth statement asked whether it is possible to replace almost all the products currently placed with sustainable alternatives. Agreement had to be expressed on a 1–7 scale where endpoints were defined as strongly disagree (1) and strongly agree (7). The rationale for the inclusion of these questions comes from the Amendment presented to MiFID2's suitability questionnaire that suggests considering sustainable preferences only after the investment goals and horizon have been discussed with a client. The literature reviewed has shown that sustainable investors are more prone to specific biases that deal with risk aversion and losses, which suggested that there might exist a feedback loop between risk and sustainable preferences that the regulatory framework does not see.

Question 2 elicited an opinion on which percentage of sustainable products composes the portfolio of the sustainable investors according to the opinion of the advisors that completes the survey. In principle the regulation suggests that the minimum amount of sustainable investment in a portfolio is a matter to be discussed with the client, without providing indications as to given percentages. This level is then used to ask which socio-economic and demographic characteristics are more likely to be found in this sustainable investor reminding the responder of the exact percentage stated at the previous question (Question 3). The list of characteristics has been taken from related findings in the empirical literature on sustainable investments: namely, we ask about the relevance of being male, a millennial, more wealthy or educated, or confident in one's financial abilities—all factors whose relevance has been discussed in Chapters 3 and 4.

Question 4 focuses on the advisors' perceptions about the volatility of sustainable products. A previous chapter has shown that empirical evidence points to sustainable mutual funds showing more stability than conventional funds.

Question 5 is the last question of this section and looks at the relevance of greenwashing in clients' concerns: it provides a short definition of greenwashing and offers three alternatives to choose from, including the option that clients are not aware of the problems, the option they are aware and thus expect more information about sustainable products and the fact that they are aware but trust the advisor to provide all the necessary information. The rationale for this question is that greenwashing risk is a key motivation for the introduction of the EU Taxonomy, aimed at providing clearly defined categories of sustainable investment. In particular, the Sustainable Finance Disclosure Regulation (SFDR) aimed at using disclosure as a means to avoid greenwashing (although the current classification has raised some doubts regarding the greenness of all Article 8 sustainable funds) and the Corporate Sustainability Reporting Directive (CSRD), which focuses on sustainable corporate processes, provides useful information to define sustainability ratings and assessments. Although not all targeted to the final investors, all the above information flows are filtered by other financial actors for them: advisors need to be aware of corporate processes and understand and be able to describe the sustainability features of their financial products. Thus, understanding the perception of clients regarding this problem is key to justify this increased information flow, avoid cognitive overload, and devise efficient communication strategies.

1.2.3 Robo Advisory and Open Finance

This section includes three questions on robo advisory and two questions on the theme of Open Finance.

The first question regarding robo advisory replicates the framework of Question 3 of the sustainable-finance section and focuses on the features of the digital investor. After providing context for the question with some information on fintech and the mention of robo-advisory, respondents are asked to rate from 1 to 7 (where, again, 1 corresponds to total disagreement and 7 to complete agreement) the likelihood that the digital investor has some features. The feature list is the same as in Question 3 and is drawn from the relevant empirical literature analyzed in the previous chapters.

Question 2 focuses on the differences between traditional in-person advisory and robo advisory, asking respondents to express their opinion (over the usual 1–7 scale) regarding some characteristics of traditional advisory (e.g., cost, accessibility, customization, etc.) drawn from the relevant literature on the features of robo advisory. The rationale is to understand whether robo advisory is seen as a direct competitor (characteristics in line with that of traditional advisory) or not.

Question 3 asks respondents to state whether robo advisory is regulated in a more stringent way than traditional advisory or not. Current regulation treats the two types of advisories in a consistent way, and we were interested in understanding whether traditional advisors are aware of the fact or are somehow biased toward robo advisory.

The last 2 questions explore the world of Open Finance and leave the domain of formal regulations to embrace a more speculative approach. Question 4 lists all possible sources of information that might become accessible to financial actors in an open framework similar to that created with the Payment and Services Directive 2 (PSD2). Respondents are asked to rank the usefulness of these different types of information for performing their fiduciary duties as advisors. The list of information ranges from banking information to other information currently not shareable outside the bank domains (with the restrictions that apply in different countries in terms of credit rating processes) such as the outstanding long-term financing of potential portfolio clients and has been devised including as many different types of information as possible. Question 5 is the only open-ended question and asks to submit any suggestions for further types of information that were not included in the previous list.

1.2.4 Socio-Demographic Characteristics

The socio-demographic section includes a question on gender, age, professional age, professional role, country where the participant worked in, and education. While these features are going to be useful to stratify respondents (e.g., education, age, or gender), some have some interesting dimensions on their own. In particular, the professional roles span across different key players in the financial field from bank employees to different forms of advisors and banks. Since these actors are all going to be affected in different ways from the discussed change, it might be interesting to see what their current perceptions are. The country in which respondents work might clarify whether, despite the harmonization efforts, some national specificities still linger and affect perceptions about these important changes. Professional age might be useful to understand to which regulatory changes the respondents have had to work through, in order to factor in the possible effect of having developed one's professional experience in a pre or post-MiFID world.

2 Survey Results

2.1 Participants Overview

The questionnaire was launched on June 7, 2022, and closed on June 16, 2022 on the Qualtrics platform and was distributed online through direct contacts and professional LinkedIn profiles of the authors. In total 77 people participated in the survey.[1] Females represent 11.69% of the sample (9 individuals), the average age is 47.8 years old (with a standard deviation equal to 13 years), and the professional age is 20.7 years (with a standard deviation equal to 12 years); unsurprisingly age and professional age are highly positively and significantly correlated.[2] Overall, 45% of the sample holds a high school diploma or a lower qualification, almost 38% hold a bachelor's degree and 15% a master's degree or other professional qualification. Both age and professional age are negatively and

[1] The survey was available in three languages: Italian, French, and English. Overall, 68 individuals completed it in Italian, 8 in English, and 2 in French. The dataset was cleaned to remove missing data and wrong imputation (words instead of numbers) that made the answer impossible to code (7 questionnaires were dropped because of these reasons).

[2] The correlation is 0.87 significant for a confidence interval equal to 0.95.

significantly correlated with education, which suggests that older individuals tend to be less educated but seem to have substituted education with on-field qualification through a longer professional experience. In fact, the negative correlation between education and professional experience is both stronger in magnitude (–0.31% versus –0.28%) and slightly more statistically significant (p-value = 0.0048 versus 0.0068). Regarding the professional role, 39% of the sample is composed of independent (21%) and non-independent (18%) financial advisors, followed by 18% bank employees, 13% asset managers, 9% analysts, and 2% academics. The remaining 9% picked the category "other" and includes one salesperson, one insurance consultant, business consultants, finance experts, and managers. The largest category, financial advisors, is largely educated, with over 72% of individuals with a bachelor's or master's degree. The following looks at the entire sample including all professional categories.

2.2 *Sustainable Finance*

The answers to the first question are detailed in Fig. 1, which includes the average and standard deviation for each element of the question and shows that participants tend to broadly agree with the attitude taken by the European regulators: most investment products can be substituted with sustainable alternatives and there are no particular red flags when it comes to specific levels risk tolerance, investment horizon, and loss tolerance of clients. There is a statistically significant positive correlation between the beliefs regarding loss aversion and risk tolerance (0.67, p-value = 0.000) and investment horizon (0.68, p-value = 0.000), showing that individuals that tend to give higher scores in one do so also in the others. There is a positive and significant correlation between age and the belief that a sustainable alternative can be found, no effect of gender (probably due to the limited number of women in the pool) or of education levels (Fig. 1).

The mean amount of sustainable investment to define the sustainable portfolio is 58% (s.d. 12%); this amount is positively correlated with the belief regarding the possibility to substitute all investments with sustainable alternatives and negatively correlated with the belief that some risk tolerance and loss aversion make sustainable investment unsuitable to some investors and with education (all results are statistically significant).

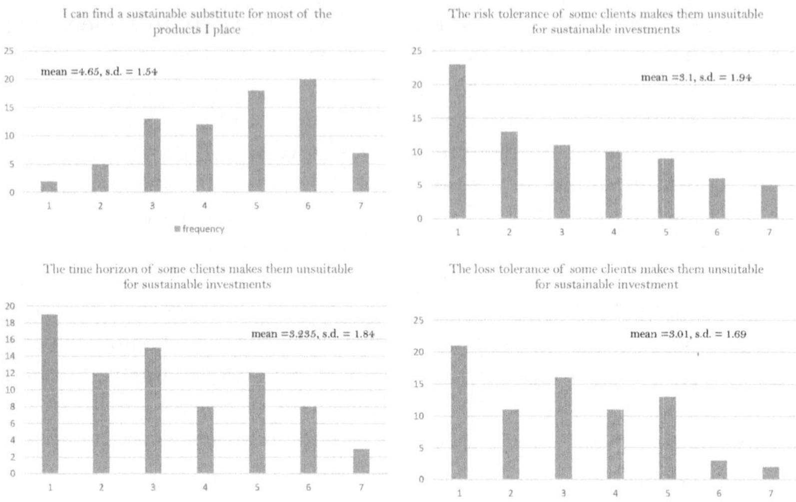

Fig. 1 Sustainability and relevant sustainability concerns

Moving on to the features of the sustainable investor,[3] results show a slightly different picture with respect to the one that emerged from empirical analyses presented in Chapter 3: given that the scale was expressed on a 7-point scale, scores over 4 tend to show agreement with the item presented on average, consistently with the literature, the sustainable investor is more likely a millennial (mean = 4.73, s.d. = 1.766921), someone who talks often about sustainability (mean = 5.17, s.d. = 1.66). Moreover, and still in line with the literature, the sustainable investor has higher income (mean = 4.38, s.d. = 1.75), education (mean = 4.5, s.d. = 1.71), financial literacy (mean = 5.04, s.d. = 1.71), and is more likely to have a positive perception about his or her competences in financial matters (mean 4.10, s.d. = 1.72).

Differently from the literature, the sustainable investor according to the sample is not necessarily male (mean = 3.16, s.d. = 1.74), and the possibility that he/she may have received an inheritance is not relevant, despite the literature calls for the difference between windfall money and earned money in dealing with risk. Moreover, the presence

[3] This investor is defined subjectively suing the percentage given by each subject at the previous question.

of economic dependencies does not seem to be a motive for sustainable investment (mean = 3.91, s.d. = 1.76). The most significant correlation scores link positively and significantly holding a university degree, having high literacy, being wealthy, and feeling competent; the correlation between having high financial literacy and feeling competent is particularly interesting, especially because the literature has established that feeling competent is crucial for both men and women in affecting risk tolerance.

The next question addressed the perceived volatility of sustainable investment with respect to a comparable unsustainable alternative; the literature did not provide consistent evidence regarding the over- or underperformance of sustainable investment nor about its riskiness. Participants overwhelmingly converge toward the perception that sustainable investment is equally volatile (56%) as opposed to less (27%) or more (17%). Interestingly, this choice variable does not significantly correlate with any of the socio-demographic information regarding the participants but shows a mild positive and significant correlation with thinking that there is a sustainable alternative for most investment products (29%, p-value = 0.0099). The amount of sustainable investment in the prototypical sustainable portfolio is not correlated in any significant way.

The last question in this section concerns the perception clients have about the issue of greenwashing. The most frequent answer in the sample is that most clients are not even aware of the problem (45.5%), while 32.5% consider that clients are aware of its existence but are not concerned about it because they trust the professional to take care of it and 22% claim that clients are aware of it and demand more information precisely to deal with their concerns. It is interesting to look at which professional figures are more likely to provide each answer: among financial advisors, independent financial advisors converge on the same relative standings, with clients being unaware of greenwashing attracting 62.5% of the preferences. Non-independent advisors still prefer the option of client unawareness (50%) but pick clients being aware and demanding more information as the second most chosen option (29%), with clients being aware but reassured by advisors at 21%. The other large group of professionals, bank employees, picks again client unawareness as the most preferred option (57%), with the other two options tying with 23% of the preferences each. This evidence suggests that despite greenwashing is a key concern at the basis of the European regulation, practitioners feel that clients are not aware of the problem. No significant correlations are found between this question and other questions relating to sustainability perceptions.

2.3 Robo Advisory and Open Finance

This section opens with a question aimed at building the profile of the technological investor that might be interested in robo advisory according to the perception of participants. Once again, each characteristic had to be rated on a 1–7 scale, thus scores over 4 points in a feature indicate that the responders consider it more likely present than not. Consistently with what found in the literature, the investor interested in robo advisory is more likely male (although the mean score is very close to 4), very likely a millennial (mean = 4.97, s.d. = 1.75), and someone who uses the app to access banking services rather than going in person (mean = 4.78, s.d. = 1.97) and who is highly financially educated (mean = 4.78, s.d. = 1.67) and perceives himself as highly financially competent (mean = 4 44.48, s.d. = 1.6). The ideal robo-advisory client is also more likely to be overconfident (mean = 4.3, s.d. = 1.95) and have a limited budget (mean = 4.34, s.d. = 2.05), not have a low tolerance for risk (mean = 2.75, s.d. = 1.48) or low experience in investing (mean = 3.02, s.d. = 1.61). Once again, the possibility that having received an inheritance might impact risk profiles and investment behavior is not considered relevant by participants (mean = 2.81, s.d. = 1.58) and given the likelihood that he is a millennial also the option "being retired" and "having economic dependencies" are not considered relevant features of the robo-advisory client.

Exploring whether some characteristics of the respondents might have explained these views, we run a series of correlation test and nonparametric tests with the following results. The opinions regarding the key features of the robo-advisory client are generally not significantly correlated with age, gender, education, or professional age of the respondents. The only exception is whether clients have low financial experience, which turns out to be significantly and negatively correlated with professional age. The professional role of participants affects the view regarding whether the ideal robo-advisory client has low tolerance for risk (Krusal-Wallis test, Chi2 = 13.77, p = 0.03) and the position regarding the inheritance (Kruskal-Wallist test, Chi2 = 17.294, p = 00083). Regarding the role of inheritance, bank employees present a more dispersed view: all scores are attributed, while for independent (non-independent) financial advisors the highest score attributed is a 5 (4) but 56% (86%) attribute scores equal to 1 or 2. Also regarding being a retiree, bank employees and independent financial advisors have more dispersed views: despite in both groups the majority of participants attribute to being a retiree a very low score (71% of independent financial advisors attribute a score lower or equal than 3, while 81% of bank employees do the same), there are some individuals that attribute the maximum score (7). Instead, 100% of non-independent advisors attribute a score lower or equal than 3.

The next question looked at how traditional financial advisory is seen as different than robo advisory in terms of a set of given characteristics: looking at mean scores, traditional advisory is seen as easier to understand (mean = 4.67, s.d. = 1.73), easier to personalize (mean = 4.88, s.d. = 2.12), and most importantly reassuring (mean = 5.038961, s.d. = 2), while participants do not agree with the fact that it may be more independent, trustworthy, easier to access, or cheaper (all mean scores are lower than 3). Kruskal–Wallis test does not find significant statistical differences across professional groups, nor any significant correlation is found among opinions regarding these characteristics and socio-economic variables (including professional qualification). Looking at the scores provided within each professional group, we observe a lot of heterogeneity in opinions (the extreme scores 1 and 7 are used within all groups). Since we do not collect any information about the features of the professional experience of the participants, we cannot draw any major conclusions regarding the views expressed. Nevertheless, the opinion regarding the key strengths of traditional advisory is shared among groups and not specific to groups that might be more targeted by the competition with robo advisory.

The next question confirmed that most of the sample is aware that robo advisory is broadly regulated in the same way as traditional advisory (over 58% of participants). This choice is not explained by any socio-demographic characteristics or depends on professional role, which confirms that the financial professionals involved in the study have up to date. In particular, 11 out of 16 independent advisors select the option that robo and traditional advisory are regulated in the same way; 9 out of 14 non-independent advisors, 7 of 14 bank employees, and 6 out of 14 wealth managers do the same.

The last questions of the questionnaire left behind the realm of the regulation to venture into the yet unknown possibility that Open Finance

bank employees		independent fin. advisors		non-independent fin. advisors		wealth managers	
securities investment	3.07	securities investment	3.31	securities investment	2.57	securities investment	3.6
real estate loans	3.92	savings	3.87	other asset management	3.78	insurance policies	3.7
savings	4	insurance policies	4.18	savings	4.21	other asset management	3.7
other asset management	4.35	other asset management	4.18	insurance policies	4.28	other unmanaged savings	4.3
consumer loans	4.71	real estate loans	4.37	other unmanaged savings	4.35	savings	4.5
insurance policies	4.78	other unmanaged savings	4.5	real estate loans	4.78	real estate loans	4.6
other unmanaged savings	5.21	consumer loans	5.75	consumer loans	5.64	long term loans	5.6
long term loans	5.93	long term loans	5.81	long term loans	6.35	consumer loans	6

Fig. 2 Information that may be useful in BETTER dealing with clients in an Open-Finance framework

may bring about. The next question asked to rank a list of possible information that may become available in an open-finance framework and its results are summarized in Fig. 2, which reports the final rank (from most useful to least useful piece of information) by professional figure, focusing on the largest categories of respondents: bank employees, financial advisors (independent and not independent), and wealth managers. The figure also reports the average rank by category attributed to each item.

Even though all these professional figures provide services that are not completely homogenous, we observe convergence on the extremes of the ranking, with all categories choosing securities investment as the most interesting information and long-term loans as the least or next to least favorite one.

The last question allowed to further comment on Open Finance and suggests other sources of information that might be relevant if they became available to all financial actors. Only 14 participants decided to answer his question and while most of them highlighted information about existing products (e.g., complementary pension plans, leasing, annual savings rate, crypto investment) other requested information that is currently available only in some instances and to some players (e.g., *Centrale Rischi*, which is the national credit information repository in Italy, normally accessible to banks and financial institutions regarding current and potential clients) or information that is not currently available (e.g., criminal records) or not yet existent (ESG rating of the different clients).

Box 1 The practitioner's view: In this box, Giuseppe Amitrano (WieldMore Investment Management) comments the results of the survey according to his perspective as a market operator and highlights the challenges that his firm is facing in promoting sustainability investments to his clients and facing the potential competition of technology and robo advisory

What do the results of this survey mean to you?

Looking at the suitability section, the results reported in Fig. 1 show few differences, testifying to the fact that the ESG theme is still to be tackled correctly among practitioners. A fact on which almost all participants in the survey tend to agree is that the customer's ability to tolerate losses does not appear to jeopardize the choice of recommending sustainable products to customers. On the contrary, this could have a positive effect for this purpose. In fact, the use of sustainable filters could end up providing an extra layer of scrutiny for the product issuers, this way reducing further the eventual risk of downside, for reputational or market reasons.

Of particular interest is the approach of clients to greenwashing concerns emerging from this survey. The fact that there is a convergence of opinions that clients are not prepared to understand the greenwashing risk explains the efforts for introducing the EU Taxonomy regulation to appropriately define which economic activities can be considered environmentally sustainable. Despite the good intentions and after introducing, along the same lines, two other important regulations, the Sustainable Finance Disclosure Regulation (SFDR) and the Corporate Sustainability Reporting Directive (CSRD), it is clear that we are still missing a clear-cut definition of the regulatory perimeter and the legal consequences of trespassing it.

Furthermore, and this is very recurrent in our discussions with colleagues and clients, there is still a lot of confusion on what is right or wrong, in or out, in our accounting and measuring of sustainable and not sustainable investments. The press is genuinely in the midst despite the importance of the topic as it is evident from an article appeared on June 15, 2022 in the Financial Times that titled: "*EU lawmakers rebel against green label for gas and nuclear.*"

The embarrassment this time is caused by the public refusal of EU lawmakers to endorse parts of the bloc's climate agenda with regard to labeling gas and nuclear as green investments to be included in the taxonomy of the European Commission.

It is evident at this point how vital is to be able to address this grey area and to finally provide investment managers with the capability to quantitatively define and measure ESG score and risk to implement all available products that effectively mitigate or enhance ESG risk and improve the overall ESG impact. Portfolio managers in the future will need to be able to:

- accurately define the ESG impact of their portfolio,
- hedge ESG risk from current investments with low ESG scores through various strategies,
- improve the overall ESG impact of their portfolio.

With regard to open finance, apart from some notable differences in the drafting of the rankings, it is interesting how all categories of professionals are aligned on the fact that open banking could bring advantages in terms of accessibility not only to current accounts, but also to investments and policies, which would make reporting and the providing of a full spectrum of customer service much easier. On the other hand, there might be cause for concern on the accessibility of data relating to short and long-term loans, which, however, can have an important impact on the recommendations in terms of financial planning and budgeting for families.

There are certainly some areas of intervention that are important for what concerns technology. In general, open banking can bring great opportunities to the world of securities, where Europe lags behind the British institutions and the US market. At the same time there are several regulatory and competition aspects that must be considered. In any case, albeit slowly, this is the way forward, as other markets have already demonstrated this process can take a few years.

While waiting for the regulator to accelerate this transformation, the Fintech ecosystem moves at a speed that is perhaps too high for the regulators (just think of what happens in terms of crypto-assets and de-fi regulation) in a way this resembles the formal process we have experienced all times.

How is your company facing the challenge of sustainability? How are regulators, technology, and markets actingto address the problem of greenwashing?

ESG-compliant investments have come to the forefront of worldwide debate and, consequently, among all market players.

For fund managers and investment professionals like us at WieldMore, this represents an array of new challenges which we must adapt to. One of the most prominent features is that ESG investments will inevitably account for a larger portion of our total portfolio and thus, ESG-related risks, which were once a small feature, and now form part of a larger, more prominent risk for portfolio managers.

In parallel with the increased awareness and demand for ESG investments, fund managers are now (or in the near future will be) subject to increased ESG disclosure requirements in both the UK & EU, via Task Force on Climate-Related Financial Disclosure Requirements (TCFR) and Sustainable Finance Disclosure Regulation (SFDR), respectively.

As a result, it's crucial that fund managers can accurately measure, understand, and explain the ESG impact of all their portfolio constituents, including derivatives to address the risk of greenwashing.

In response to this dynamic shift in the investment management landscape, regulators and market players aim to empower investors with the ability to assess ESG risks, implement more conscious ESG investment decisions and disclose their ESG impact to relevant stakeholders.

There is nowadays a very strong focus on achieving these goals through the implementation of a regulatory framework but also technological advancements capable of measuring the ESG impact of products, which are currently not in the scope of ESG assessment since the market has not provided all the answers to analyze the whole ESG portfolio impact.

A clear example is given by the derivative market, as there are around €244tn in market value of derivatives in the EU which are not assessed in terms of ESG impact.

It is becoming more and more imperative for fund managers to be able to assess and measure the ESG impact of all products both from a risk and a contractually legal point of view.

This is a first step toward winning over greenwashing.

A more quantitative disclosure of the ESG impact will allow investment managers, whose mandates and clients' demands are increasingly shifting toward ESG-related objectives, to assess ESG risks, implement better ESG conscious investment decisions and successively disclose their ESG impact and ESG risk mitigation strategy to relevant stakeholders.

In the United Kingdom, the Government is suggesting three major actions to allow the transition to greener investments:

1. informing investors and consumers, to easily identify, assess, and present the client's portfolio in terms of its ESG impact;
2. acting on this information, i.e., developing ESG scoring and proprietary algorithm to help design strategies, derivatives, and assets allocation to optimize the overall ESG impact of the client's portfolio;

3. shifting financial flows, from investments negatively impacting the world in terms of ESG factors to investments with a positive ESG impact, thus realizing a real green transition.

How is your company dealing with the supposed threatof Fintech and roboadvisory?

In our experience as a young startup company and an authorized and supervised financial institution, we came across a series of practical issues that have affected our daily activity and put pressure on us to come up with more efficient solutions in order to depart from the traditional in-person financial advisory service. For this reason, to be more productive and "cost savvy", we have tried to improve our tech capabilities, focusing on improving the performance of suitability and risk profiling. We have then identified few relevant needs for innovation in the market of advisory:

(1) appropriate and suitable savings and pension advice could improve everyone's life. Yet only 1 in 10 adults in the United Kingdom received advice in 2020 and *1/5 of advice received was unsuitable* (https://www.fca.org.uk/publication/multi-firm-reviews/assessing-suitability-review.pdf), resulting in numerous complaints addressed to *the Financial Ombudsman* (https://www.financial-ombudsman.org.uk/businesses/complaints-deal/investments/assessing-suitability-investments). There are *8.4 mln un-advised adults with investible assets between £10,000–£150,000* (https://www.fca.org.uk/publication/corporate/evaluation-of-the-impact-of-the-rdr-and-famr.pdf).

(2) 60% of professionally managed investment portfolios are *likely unsuitable or their risk assessment is unclear* (https://www.fca.org.uk/publication/thematic-reviews/tr15-12.pdf), i.e., £5 trillion of financial and pension wealth is at risk of being inapt and causes financial harm (https://www.ons.gov.uk/peoplepopulationandcommunity/personalandhouseholdfinances/incomeandwealth/bulletins/totalwealthingreatbritain/latest).

A very similar picture is present in the rest of Europe.

The *advice gap* (https://www.fca.org.uk/publication/corporate/famr-final-report.pdf), captures the fact that many people who could benefit from financial advice are not receiving it. The second issue is that advice and allocated investment portfolios do not accurately correspond with the customers' risk profile. Consequently, the FCA's incoming 2021 *New*

Consumer Duty (https://www.fca.org.uk/news/press-releases/fca-introduce-new-consumer-duty-drive-fundamental-shift-industry-mindset) further requires firms "to offer products and service that are fit for purpose." Technological advancements in this case are neither creating a problem to traditional advisory business nor posing a threat to the main street banking business model. Rather technology here can help reduce the advice gap by either creating solutions that enable customers to directly access automated investment support via robo advisors or by increasing the financial advisers' capacity and lowering their costs to make their services affordable for more customers and to enable them to get customers with smaller savings on board. For a small company like ours with clear constraints on resources this is the only solution.

Regulations require advisers to measure suitability at least annually through evaluation of a risk profiling questionnaire answered by the retail customer. This aims to capture their investment goals, level of financial knowledge, and attitudes toward investment losses. Followed by an interview, the adviser determines which investments match their risk profile and objectives. Not only are the manual questionnaires time-consuming to fill in, but at least 2/3 are not best placed for the assessment due to a lack of questions regarding the customers' personal characteristics, although state-of-the-art research in behavioral economics has shown the value of such questions when creating risk profiles. Some institutions have adopted riskier and more expensive solutions, which include some personal characteristic questions within their assessment. However, these solutions do not monitor life changes, automate assessments, or provide auto-matching of suitable investments. This is a very important feature when it comes to winning the confidence and trust of investors to make sure they are willing to rely on automated financial services.

But is the riskiness of using robo advisors the same as of using in-person advisors? Well, this depends pretty much on the level of control and regulatory requirements needed to perform the above-described functions. In our case, for example, there is a significant further legal barrier as this activity requires financial authorization that not all companies possess. In response to the needs highlighted, we have tried adopting a cost-efficient, cutting-edge suitability assessment and portfolio matching tool. This allows us to both scale up our offerings and reach out to other clients.

The application of the most recent technologies, with the latest advancements in machine learning (ML) and AI present new forms of portfolio customization previously unavailable, enabling us to provide more cost-efficient, tailored solutions.

With the help of a more dynamic suitability assessment tool, it is possible to make sure individuals' risk tolerance is not affected in the process, while at the same time radically improving all stages of investment suitability compliance, by:

- defining an intelligent risk profile evaluation formula balancing circumstances and investment goals and raising biases typical for the customer's profile to the attention of the adviser.
- creating better questionnaire that takes all relevant socio-economic and behavioral circumstances into account based on scientific research.
- using transfer Learning to train ML to make optimal suitability assessments based on aggregated data of adviser decisions. This automation can enable resource-efficient profile re-calculations, paving the way for more dynamic assessments and consequential portfolio adjustments while saving time and lowering compliance costs.
- suggesting a fine-tuned match between the risk profile, goals, values, and possible portfolios of investments.

3 Final Discussion and Conclusions

This chapter presented the results of a survey shared with financial professionals and regarding the future challenges affecting the profession of portfolio management and advice provision. The motivation for the survey was to provide the pulse of the post-MiFID2 debate regarding the two key challenges that were identified in Chapters 3 and 4—sustainable investment and Fintech with robo advisory.

The path taken in this book has shown that even if financial risk tolerance has always been a key component in the determination of the propensity to invest and the portfolio compositions of individual investors, the official regulation in Europe left behind scientific findings for some years before introducing a formal tool—the suitability questionnaire with MiFID. Despite the European regulators were clearly moving in the right direction, the applicability and functionality of the early questionnaire have been disputed by both practitioners and empirical literature. With MiFID2 the regulator has moved forward in improving the idea of suitability, contaminating it with ideas coming from behavioral finance (e.g., loss aversion) but forgetting that excessive information might trigger other behavioral responses. The Covid-19 crisis has basically halted the development of a formal successor to MiFID2 but the European regulator has moved forward in a series of other directions that complement and change some of the original MiFID2 prescriptions. The European Action Plan for Sustainable Future of the European Union laid out important new ground rules that affect the way in which clients are known and their preferences accounted for in the final advice/portfolio allocation. The current challenge now is represented by the introduction of sustainability preferences within suitability questionnaires in an effective way: only if individual investors truly prefer sustainable products, the increased costs for improved and transparent corporate processes and sustainability disclosure will pay off for firms.

The other open challenge that financial institutions and investors are facing is represented by the upsurge of Fintech and robo-advisory services, which impose traditional banks and financial institutions to rethink their business models. Technology represents either an opportunity or a threat, as the academic literature has thoroughly highlighted. On a regulatory ground, the PSD2 Directive (2016) has paved the way for an increased competition in the market, introducing, among other novelties, Open Banking and its natural evolution, Open Finance. In such an environment, investors' protection implies to consider new "threats," like for example data protection, a correct risk profiling in case of use of robo-advisory services, a supervision of the algorithms that match investors' risk profile with an investment recommendation. In this regard, the Regulator has revised the Guidelines on Suitability in 2018 to consider these new players. However, it is still not clear if and how investors' risk tolerance possibly changes when using automated financial services and to what extent the Regulator can increase investors' protection and the suitability of the services offered.

Appendix: The Questionnaire

Welcome! This is a survey on the challenges and opportunities in financial advisory in the post-MiFID2 regulatory landscape.

The survey is anonymous. We will only ask you for some demographic information for statistical purposes, which however will not allow us to trace your identity. We ask you to answer all questions spontaneously and sincerely. Answering the questions will take about 10 min.

Thank you for the help you are giving to research!

Q1 The European commission has introduced a series of regulatory changes aimed at stimulating the diffusion of sustainable investments. think about your current clients and their portfolios and how you are or will be facing the challenge of sustainable finance.

For each of the statements below, indicate to what extent you agree or disagree (1 = strongly disagree; 7 = completely agree).

	1	*2*	*3*	*4*	*5*	*6*	*7*
I can find a sustainable substitute for most of the products I place ()							
The risk tolerance of some clients makes them unsuitable for sustainable investments ()							
The time horizon of some clients makes them unsuitable for sustainable investments ()							
The loss tolerance of some clients makes them unsuitable for sustainable investments ()							

Q2 In your opinion, what percentage of sustainable investments out of the total managed portfolio defines a "sustainable portfolio"? indicate the percentage (e.g., x%) in the box below.

Q3 In your opinion and experience which of the following characteristics identify the **ideal client profile to offer sustainable investments (portfolio with [the percentage entered at the previous question of sustainable financial products).**

For each of the statements below, indicate to what extent you agree or disagree (1 = strongly disagree; 7 = completely agree).

	1	*2*	*3*	*4*	*5*	*6*	*7*
Is male							
Is under 41 years old							
Financially supports one or more people (spouse, children, parents, etc.)							
Is retired							
Often talks about sustainable investments both in the environment and in society							
Recently received an inheritance							
Has an above-average level of financial literacy							
Has a high income level							
Has an academic degree							
Feels competent in financial investments							

Q4 In your experience, given the same financial product, sustainable investments (as opposed to the unsustainable ones) are

○ less volatile
○ equally volatile
○ more volatile

Q5 In the European Action Plan for sustainability, the European Commission has proposed to carry out numerous actions to produce sustainability standards, certifications, and labels to be applied to sustainable financial products. The aim of these actions is to fight greenwashing, i.e., the practice by which some companies present themselves or their financial products as sustainable when they in fact are not.

In your experience, what is the investors' stance as regards the greenwashing problem?

o it is an issue they are not familiar with
o it is an issue they are familiar with and thus they are particularly careful about sustainable investments documentation
o it is an issue they know exists but do not worry about because they trust that the products I propose are not affected by it

Section 2—Robo advisory and open finance

Q6 For some years now, the European Commission has been considering the digitization of financial services, which concerns not only information on services and products but also all new digital services such as fully or partially automated advisory (robo advisory).

In your opinion and experience, which of the following characteristics identify **the profile of the client interested in a robo-advisory service in a context where the service may not replace traditional advisory, but rather be offered alongside it.**

For each of the statements below, indicate to what extent you agree or disagree (1 = strongly disagree; 7 = completely agree).

	1	*2*	*3*	*4*	*5*	*6*	*7*
Is male							
Is under 41 years old							

(continued)

(continued)

	1	*2*	*3*	*4*	*5*	*6*	*7*
Financially supports one or more people (spouse, children, parents, etc.)							
Is retired							
Accesses their bank account only via online app							
Recently received an inheritance							
Has a low risk tolerance							
Has an above-average level of financial literacy							
Feels competent in financial investments							
Has little financial experience							
Has high self-confidence							
Has financial resources of less than 500,000 euros							

Q7 What Makes a Traditional (In-Person) Advisory Service Different from that of a Robo Advisor?

For each of the statements below, indicate to what extent you agree or disagree (1 = strongly disagree; 7 = completely agree).

	1	2	3	4	5	6	7
It is cheaper ()							
It is more easily accessible ()							
It is easier to understand ()							
It is more reliable ()							
It is more customized to the client ()							
It is more independent ()							
It is more reassuring ()							

Q8 Compared to financial advisors authorized to operate in the european union, robo advisors are subject to…

○ fewer regulations
○ the same regulations
○ more regulations

Q9 Imagine an Open-Finance System Akin to that Set Forth by the PSD2 Directive on Open Banking Will Be Developed. Open Finance is a Voluntary Data Sharing Model in Which Financial Information is Shared.

The following list includes financial information that you may want to have access to for dealing with your client's needs better. Sort such information from the most to the least useful

______ outstanding consumer loans.
______ outstanding existing real estate loans.

______ insurance policies.
______ other medium/long-term loans.
______ securities investments.
______ savings.
______ other forms of asset management.
______ other forms of unmanaged savings.

Q10 Is there any type of information you would like to have access to in an open-finance system which is not included in the list above? if there is, please enter it below.

Section 3—Socio-demographic section

Before concluding, we would like you to answer some questions for statistical purposes.

Q11 Indicate your gender.

○ Male (1)
○ Female (2)

Q12 Indicate your age in numbers (e.g., 25).

Q13 Indicate your professional age * in numbers (e.g., 15).

*Number of years you have been employed in the banking or financial sector

Q14 Indicate the professional role you currently hold.

○ Bank employee
○ Independent financial advisor
○ Financial advisor

- o Analyst
- o Asset or wealth manager
- o Academic (lecturer, researcher, or professor)
- o Other (specify) ______________________________

Q15 Please select the country in which you currently work.

- o Italy
- o France
- o United Kindgom
- o Another European country (please state which one)
- o An extra-European country (please state which one)

Q16 Indicate the highest degree you hold

- o Primary school diploma
- o Middle School diploma
- o High school diploma
- o College/University Degree
- o Masters or other professional graduate school
- o Ph.D.

Index

© The Author(s), under exclusive license to Springer Nature Switzerland AG 2022

C. Cruciani et al., *Understanding Financial Risk Tolerance*,
https://doi.org/10.1007/978-3-031-13131-8

The manufacturer's authorised representative in the EU is Springer Nature Customer Service Centre GmbH, Europaplatz 3, 69115 Heidelberg, Germany. If you have any concerns regarding our products, please contact ProductSafety@springernature.com

Printed and bound by CPI Group (UK) Ltd, Croydon, CR0 4YY
30/09/2026
02225490-0003